TEACHING AND PERFORMING RENAISSANCE CHORAL MUSIC

A Guide for Conductors and Performers

FRANCES R. POE

The Scarecrow Press, Inc.
Metuchen, N.J., & London
1994

This book is based in part on Chapters III and IV of the author's dissertation, "The Development of Instructional Materials for Teaching and Performing Renaissance Choral Music," accepted by the faculty of the Graduate School as partial fulfillment of the requirements for the degree of Doctor of Philosophy, Indiana University, Bloomington, Indiana, 1978.

British Library Cataloguing-in-Publication data available

Library of Congress Cataloging-in-Publication Data

Poe, Frances R., 1937-
    Teaching and performing renaissance choral music : a guide for conductors and performers / Frances R. Poe.
        p.   cm.
    Includes bibliographical references (p.   ).
    ISBN 0-8108-2778-6. — ISBN 0-8108-2886-3 (pbk.) (alk. paper)
    1. Choral singing—Instruction and study. 2. Choral conducting. 3. Performance practice (Music)—15th century. 4. Performance practice (Music)—16th century. 5. Performance practice (Music)—17th century. I. Title.
MT875.P55   1994
782.5'143—dc20   93-23597

To the memory of my mother, Frances Castleberry Poe,
and in honor of those students who inspire me
with their quest for excellence

Table of Contents

The Performer's Workbook

Preface

In a time when critical thinking is advocated at all levels of education, the choral class is no exception. Therefore, the purpose of this material is twofold: (1) to provide students in choral ensembles with a representative sampling of Renaissance choral music and information about its style and structure, and (2) to provide choral conductors with instructional materials which can help them teach students about the music as it is being rehearsed and prepared for performance. It is hoped that the use of this material will enable the conductor to explain more about the music itself in the time allotted for the choral class. The small choral ensemble, considered the best medium for performing Renaissance choral music, offers an ideal situation for teaching musical style and structure through the mode of performance because the participants in small ensembles usually have an above-average interest and ability in music. Nevertheless, teaching and learning musical understanding through performance will take extra effort on the part of all involved.

"The Conductor's Manual" can be used whole or in part. It is suggested that students first experience the music by either singing the selections or listening to recordings, if they are available. The conductor should then refer to the study guides in "The Conductor's Manual" and point out various aspects of the music*, which will enhance the students' knowledge of Renaissance style. Therefore, when the music is re-experienced or sung, it will be done so with increased understanding. "The Performer's Workbook" appears as the second part of this text so students will be able to study important aspects of the music outside of the rehearsal. "The Performer's Workbook" is meant to be used. For best results, it is suggested that the General Information section for each genre be taught before specific pieces are studied and performed.

I wish to especially thank my colleagues Frank Abrahams, Geraldine Ward, and Patricia Windemuth for their help and encouragement; for those who aided me in the dissertation stage of this work, Dr. Charles R. Hoffer and Professor William Dalglish. I am also grateful to the choral directors who tested these materials in their choral classes: Messrs. Ronald Berresford, Michael Imperiale, Richard Ludlum, and Edward Shiley.

I wish to also thank my family for their love and support, and Mr. Andrew Megill for his help as a choral librarian and scholar and Ms. Janet Gillespie and

---

*The use of G, g, g', g", in referring to different octaves, is used throughout this manual.

Ms. Lynn Miller for their careful preparation of this manuscript. Special thanks are also due Professor Christopher E. Grzesik and Ms. Irene Jervis for their help with the mechanical aspects of this text.

Frances R. Poe
Westminster Choir College
The School of Music of Rider College
1994

The Conductor's Manual

The French Chanson

General Information

Chanson is the French word for song. In French-speaking countries the word chanson has been used in a general way for centuries to describe any monophonic, homophonic or polyphonic song composed on a vernacular text. Collections of monophonic chansons date from as early as the twelfth century, and by the sixteenth century the polyphonic chanson had become one of the most beloved courtly musical forms in France. Jean-Jacques Rousseau, the eighteenth-century philosopher and writer, gave an apt and informative definition of the chanson in his 1768 *Dictionary of Music*: " A sort of very short lyric poem, generally upon some pleasant subject, to which an air is added so that it can be sung on intimate occasions, as at table, with one's friends, with one's sweetheart, or even when one is alone, in order for a few moments to drive away boredom if one is rich, and to help one bear misery and labour if one is poor " (p.78).

The sixteenth-century chanson can be divided into three periods and styles. In general, the earlier Netherlands chanson, while more strictly contrapuntal, is not always obviously imitative; the later chanson is characterized by imitative counterpoint. The forms of the Netherlands chanson (circa 1475-1520) vary from the fixed French monophonic chanson (*ballade, virelai, rondeau*) to those cast in throughcomposed, or free forms. The chanson of this period reached its peak in the compositions of Netherlands composer Josquin Desprez (zhoss-can day pray) (circa 1450-1521). Josquin's chansons influenced and inspired the French composers of the second chanson period who, around 1520, sought to cultivate a somewhat simpler, more homophonic design. The chief composer of this new French tradition of precision and grace was the gifted Frenchman Claudin de Sermisy (sair-mee-zee) (circa 1490-1562). After 1550 the chanson tradition was modified in France because of the overpowering influence of the Italian madrigal. Chansons of this period are in general more polyphonic than homophonic, with a lightness and gaiety achieved through the frequent use of rapid repeated notes and dancelike rhythms. French musician Guillaume Costeley (cot-lay) (1531-1606) helped to maintain the chanson tradition during the second half of the sixteenth century. Many of his chansons are considered to be among the most beautiful and refreshing of the genre.

Chanson Texts

Generally, two types of poems were used as chanson texts during the Renaissance. The first, which constitutes the majority, is simple, sentimental, somewhat stereotyped, and without much individuality. In poems of this type, love is treated idealistically, the main subjects dealing with complaints of the discarded lover to his mistress and the laments of unrequited love. Josquin's "Mille regretz" and Sermisy's "J'ay fait pour vous cent mille pas" are both examples of this poetic type. The second type emphasized the humorous aspects of male-female relationships. Many of these texts, although written by some of the best French poets, are not only frivolous but earthy as well.

The content of chanson texts is often reflected in the music. Sentimental chansons, such as those by Josquin and Sermisy, are normally written in long time values, with melismatic sections and a flowing style. Chansons employing light or humorous poems often use a "patter" technique in which words are set to rapid notes, with few melismatic passages.

Performance

The character of the poetry largely determines the tempo of the chanson. It is generally agreed that the basic pulsation (the note taking a full beat which, in this music, is usually the half note), can range from M.M. 60 to as much as 120 since there is a normal tendency to perform the more humorous chanson in a faster tempo than the sentimental type. Both types should be performed at a tempo which always allows for clear pronunciation of the words. The chanson is always rhythmic and the principal beats are accented.

Sudden changes in volume should never occur; crescendos and diminuendos should be used sparingly and executed tastefully. No passage should ever be sung so loudly that words are not clearly pronounced. If the words are not easily understood, the passage is probably too loud and not sufficiently crisp.

Most chansons are simple enough in structure to be performed by small choirs, although it should be understood that they were composed as chamber music. Pictures of singers performing secular Renaissance music always show small groups of soloists, not choirs. If several singers are used for each part, they must strive for a unified sound or the desired effect will be lost. Chansons were frequently performed on instruments alone or with one solo voice and instruments. Performances in which voices and instruments are combined are not only desirable but highly enjoyable.

"Mille regretz" ("Deep Is My Grief")

I.   Title of Composition
"Mille regretz" ("Deep Is My Grief")

II.   Type of Composition
Netherlands chanson

III. Composer
Josquin Desprez was probably born in 1450 in Picardy, that part of the lowlands which today lies on the Franco-Belgian border. He began his musical career as a choirboy and later became one of the most learned and influential musicians of his time. He traveled to Italy where he was employed by the Sforzas in Milan, the Papal Chapel in Rome, and the Duke of Ferrara. After the duke's death in 1505, Josquin returned to his homeland where he died in 1521. His compositions include seventy chansons, twenty-two Masses, numerous motets, hymns, and psalm settings. The beauty and skill found in his music caused him, even in his own day, to be called the "Father of Musicians."

IV.   Text
Both the French text and an English translation appear in the edition provided here. Texts should be read by conductor and performers for clues concerning tempo and dynamics. The indications which appear in the music are editorial (there being none in the original) and merely serve as suggestions for performance.

V.   Background
"Mille regretz" is one of Josquin's last chansons, possibly written for the Holy Roman emperor and king of Spain, Charles V, in 1520. This chanson is considered one of Josquin's most beautiful, the overall effect being one of simplicity.

VI.   Structural and Stylistic Elements

    A.   Medium
    Soprano, alto, tenor, and bass. "Mille regretz" exemplifies the change from writing parts successively, as was customary in the Middle Ages, to simultaneous composition in which all voices are conceived at once. This chanson represents the characteristic sound of four or more voices of similar character and equal importance that Renaissance composers employed for more than 150 years.

13

B. **Meter**
Duple. This chanson is cast in the dance form of a *pavane* (pah-VAHN), an Italian court dance which probably originated in Padua. It is in slow duple meter and should be performed in a dignified, ceremonial style. Josquin's use of this form shows how a court dance could be used to express pain, grief, and resignation.

C. **Tonality**
Phrygian mode.

D. **Form**
Through-composed, but a condensed summary of the first section appears at the end (compare mm. 13-17 with m. 34 to the end).

E. **Dissonances**
Some of the main dissonances, or nonharmonic tones, which were used by sixteenth-century composers appear in Josquin's "Mille regretz." They are called (1) passing tones, (2) neighbor tones, and (3) suspensions.

1. Passing tone
Usually moves on weak part of beat.
Always ascends or descends stepwise from one consonance to another.
Always continues in the direction by which it is approached.

Examples
m. 3   Passing note e' in soprano.
                       Passing note c in bass.
m. 20   Passing note c" in soprano.
                       Passing note e' in alto.
mm. 35, 37   Passing note b in tenor.
m. 39   Passing note f' in soprano.

2. Neighbor tone
Usually comes on weak part of beat. It moves stepwise, but instead of proceeding in the direction in which it started, it turns back to the note it has just left.

Examples
m. 4   Neighbor tone c' in soprano.
                       Neighbor tone a in bass.

3. Suspension
A dissonance found on *accented* part of the beat. Suspensions involved three specific steps:

a) Preparation. Always on weak beat.
b) Suspension. Always on the following strong beat.
c) Resolution. Always on the following weak beat.

P-S-R refers to the movement of a single voice part.

Examples:
m. 8   a′ in soprano is preparation tone.
m. 9   a′ in soprano is suspension.
         g′ is resolution tone.

The eighth notes in the soprano create an ornamented resolution.

mm. 11-12   Same suspension as found in mm. 8-9.

F. **Texture**
One of the most interesting aspects of Josquin's compositions is the way in which he varied the texture. The following variety appears in "Mille regretz":

1.   mm. 19-24 Soprano and alto are answered by tenor and bass (imitative duet).

2.   mm. 27-31 Soprano is answered by the alto; both voices are then answered by tenor and bass.

VII. Additional Source
Des Prez, Josquin. *Werke*. Edited by Albert Smijers. Leipzig: Kistner und Siegel, 1925.

VIII. Recordings
French Renaissance Vocal Music. La Chanson & La Danse. Musical Heritage Society, 1125. Decca-9629.

Danserye 1551. Camerata Hungarica. Hungaraton-HCD 12194-2. Stereo.

Deep Is My Grief
(Mille Regretz)
S A T B, a cappella

English Text by
Melinda Edwards

Josquin des Prez (1445-1521)
Edited by Walter Ehret

"J'ay fait pour vous cent mille pas" ("A Hundred Thousand Steps")

I. Title of Composition

"J'ay fait pour vous cent mille pas" ("A Hundred Thousand Steps")

II. Type of Composition

French chanson

III. Composer

Claudin de Sermisy (circa 1490-1562) spent most of his life in the service of the great French king Francis I. He worked as a singer, composer, and later director of the royal chapel. Sermisy was one of the most popular composers of his time, writing chanson-influenced Masses, four books of motets, a Passion, many miscellaneous works, and some 110 chansons. His music was frequently published by Pierre Attaingnant (a-tain-yun), the well-known French publisher, and appeared in numerous other sources throughout Europe.

IV. Text

Both the French text and an English translation appear in the modern edition provided here. The texts should be read by conductor and performers for clues concerning proper tempo and dynamics. The indications which appear in the music are editorial (there being none in the original) and merely serve as suggestions for performance.

V. Background

Sermisy's fame as a chanson composer comes mainly from his four-part love songs set in simple homophonic style with few imitations or melismas. The chanson "J'ay fait pour vous cent mille pas" is an excellent example of that style and type.

VI. Structural and Stylistic Elements

    A. Medium

    Soprano, alto, tenor, and bass. The soprano is the most important voice melodically; the lowest voice serves as a harmonic bass.

    B. Meter

    Duple.

C. Rhythm

Sermisy's chansons are predominantly homorhythmic; all voices move in the same rhythm except for slight variations in one or two voices.

D. Texture

When all voices move in the same rhythm, a succession of intervals or chords is produced which in turn produces a homophonic texture. Except for a slight imitative section at measure 17, the overall texture is chordal, or homophonic.

E. Text Setting

The text setting is basically syllabic, one note to each syllable of text. As a rule, homorhythm and syllabic text setting go hand in hand.

F. Mode

Ionian mode on A.

G. Cadences

Cadences which appear at the end of phrases in Sermisy's chanson are mostly V-I cadences with the scale degrees 8-7-8 in the soprano and a 2-1 descent in the tenor.

Examples
mm. 5-6.
mm. 11-12.
mm. 16-17.
mm. 24-25.

Example 2. Sermisy, "J'ay fait pour vous cent mille pas," p. 4, mm. 5-6.

These cadences show the tendency toward functional harmony in Renaissance music.

VII. Additional Source

Sermisy, Claudin de. *Corpus mensurabilis musicae 52*. Edited by G. Allaire and I. Cazeaux. Rome: American Institute of Musicology, 1970- .

J'ay fait pour vous cent mille pas

A Hundred Thousand Steps

Chanson

for Four-Part Chorus of Mixed Voices a cappella

Duration about 1 minute

English text by I. C.

Claudin de Sermisy
(c. 1490 - 1562)

Edited by Isabelle Cazeaux

A. B. 135 - 4

Copyright © 1967 by Tetra Music Corp.

Sole selling agent: Alexander Broude, Inc.

Printed in U.S.A.

Example 3. Reprinted with permission.

4

6

"Allon, gay Bergeres"
("Come, Gay Shepherds")

I.   Title of Composition

"Allon, gay Bergeres" ("Come, Gay Shepherds")

II.   Type of Composition

French chanson

III.   Composer

Guillaume Costeley (circa 1531-1606) was probably born in Normandy. He worked as a composer and organist at the courts of Henry II and Charles IX of France. Costeley was primarily a chanson composer, writing in the homophonic style established by Sermisy and in the late sixteenth-century style known as *musique mesurée*, or measured music. In *musique mesurée* the music follows the metrical rhythm of the text. Although Costeley is best known for his chansons, he also wrote a keyboard fantasy while in the service of King Charles IX.

IV.   Text

Both the French text and an English translation appear in the modern edition provided here. The texts should be read by conductor and performers for clues concerning tempo and dynamics. The indications which appear in the music are editorial (there being none in the original) and merely serve as suggestions for performance.

V.   Background

This chanson by Costeley is a noël, a popular Christmas song. Numerous collections of noëls were published during the sixteenth century which attests to the popularity of this form. Another Christmas chanson by Costeley is the beautiful "Sus, debout gentilz Pasteurs" ("Now, Arise ye Shepherds Mild"). That one, along with the one presented here, would make delightful programming during the Christmas season.

VI.   Structural and Stylistic Elements

A.   Medium

Soprano, alto, tenor, and bass.

B.   Meter

Duple.

C.   **Rhythm and Texture**

The "Allon, gay Bergeres" refrains are homorhythmic: all the voices move in the same rhythm which produces a chordal or homophonic effect. The verses are polyrhythmic: all the voices move in different rhythms and the texture is more polyphonic.

D.   **Form**

This chanson is probably one of the earliest examples of rondo form, characterized by the alternation of a recurrent refrain with various verses. The overall form is ABACADAEA.

E.   **Text Setting**

Syllabic, one note or chord to each syllable of text. As a rule, homorhythm and syllabic text setting go hand in hand.

F.   **Tonality**

Costeley begins this chanson in the Aeolian mode, or d minor, and ends in the Ionian mode, or in D major. Such changes are not typical of Renaissance music; Costeley was an innovator in this respect.

G.   **Cadences**

Costeley ends this noël with a V-I cadence. There is a raised third in the final chord which was a common practice after 1500.

VII. Additional Source

Expert, Henry, ed. *Les Maîtres musiciens de la Renaissance française.* Paris: Alphonse Leduc, 1894-1908.

VIII. Recording

Christmas Hymns and Carols, Vol. II, Robert Shaw Chorale, RCA Victor LM 1711.

COME, GAY SHEPHERDS

Come, gay shepherds,

Be joyful,

Follow me.

Come to see the King

Who, from heaven, on earth is born.

Come, gay shepherds,

Be joyful,

Follow me.

I shall make him a nice present. Of what?

Of this flute of mine, so gay.

Come, gay shepherds,

Be joyful,

Follow me.

A cake shall I give him.

And I a full bumper shall offer.

Come, gay shepherds,

Be joyful,

Follow me.

Ho, ho quiet now, I see him,

He suckles well without his thumb, the little King.

Come, gay shepherds,

Be joyful,

The King is drinking.

Allon, Gay Bergeres

For Four-Part Chorus of Mixed Voices
a cappella

Guillaume Costeley (1531-1606)
Edited by Alice Parker
and Robert Shaw

Note: Accentuation in this sixteenth-century chanson should be with the text rather than with the bar lines.

This chanson has been recorded by the Robert Shaw Chorale in RCA Victor LM 1711, Volume II of *Christmas Hymns and Carols.*

Al - lon, gay, gay, gay Ber - ge - res, al - lon, gay,

Al - lon, gay, gay, gay Ber - ge - res, al - lon, gay,

Al - lon, gay, gay, gay Ber - ge - res, al - lon, gay,

Al - lon, gay, gay, gay Ber - ge - res, al - lon, gay,

Al - lon, gay, soy - ez le - ge - res, Suy - vez moy. Un beau pre - sent

Al - lon, gay, soy - ez le - ge - res, Suy - vez moy. Un beau pre - sent

Al - lon, gay, soy - ez le - ge - res, Suy - vez moy. Un beau pre - sent luy

Al - lon, gay, soy - ez le - ge - res, Suy - vez moy.

Roy, Gay, gay. Al - lon, gay, gay, gay Ber - ge - res, al - lon, gay, Al - lon,

Roy, Gay, gay. Al - lon, gay, gay, gay Ber - ge - res, al - lon, gay, Al - lon,

— le pe-tit Roy, Al - lon, gay, gay, gay Ber - ge - res, al - lon, gay, Al - lon,

— le pe-tit Roy, Al - lon, gay, gay, gay Ber - ge - res, al - lon, gay, Al - lon,

gay, soy - ez le - ge - res, Le Roy boit, le Roy boit.

gay, soy - ez le - ge-res, Le Roy boit, le Roy boit. _____

gay, soy - ez le - ge-res, Le Roy boit, le Roy boit.

gay, soy - ez le - ge - res, Le Roy boit, le Roy boit.

The Italian Madrigal and *Balletto*

General Information

The word madrigal comes from the medieval Latin *matricale*, "a pastorale in the mother tongue." The early sixteenth-century madrigal was a fusion of the homophonic Italian *frottola* (FRAW-to-la), the French chanson, and the polyphonic imitative style of the Netherlanders. In the early history of the madrigal, only one Italian played a prominent role. He, Constanzo Festa (circa 1490-1545), competed with a group of Netherlanders, Philippe Verdelot (vaird-lo) (circa 1480-1545), Jacob Arcadelt (arr-ca-delt') (circa 1505-1560), and Adrian Willaert (vill'-lahrrt) (circa 1490-1562), in whose hands the early madrigal (1520-1550) developed to its fullest extent in Italy. Although the madrigals composed in this period are basically chordal, imitation is used to provide variety and interest.

A change of texture takes place in the madrigals of Willaert's pupil, Cipriano de Rore (ro'reh) (1516-65), whose music is basically polyphonic and imitative. Rore set no frivolous texts to music and often employed chromaticism to portray the emotions expressed in the text. He fused music and text with such skill and originality that he is considered one of the most outstanding composers of the sixteenth century. While other composers in the second madrigal period (1530-80), such as Orlando di Lasso (1532-94) and Palestrina (1525-94), were not greatly affected by Rore's use of chromaticism, those of the third and last period of the Italian madrigal were profoundly influenced.

The third period (1580-1620), often called the period of the chromatic madrigal, was a period when the search for unusual effects was often carried to the extreme. In the madrigals of Luca Marenzio (mah-rents'-yo) (1553-99), Carlo Gesualdo (jeh-zoo-ahl'-do) (circa 1560-1613) and Claudio Monteverdi (1567-1643), all sorts of dramatic effects, text painting, chromaticism, and unusual harmonies were employed without sacrificing the tradition of elaborate polyphony.

The madrigal was not the only type of secular vocal music in Italy during the sixteenth century. Several popular forms of a somewhat lighter character became prominent, the main one being the *balletto* (bah-LET-to), which was a song intended for dancing as well as singing and playing. One of its main characteristics is the use of a "fa-la" refrain. It is in a simple homophonic style, with clear major-minor harmonies and evenly phrased sections which are often repeated. Italy's leading composer of *balletti* was Giovanni Gastoldi (circa 1550-1622), whose works in this form were imitated by both English and German composers.

Italian Madrigal Texts

Many poems used as madrigal texts, especially in the early sixteenth century, were of little literary merit. Quality improved, however, due to the concern of the Venetian nobleman and scholar Cardinal Bembo (1470-1547), who sought to restore the expressiveness of the Italian language which had steadily declined after Petrarch's time in the fourteenth century. Petrarch was the model for Bembo, who saw to it that Petrarch's collection of lyric poems, the *Canzoniere*, was widely read and published. The poems in this collection, with their wide range of emotional contrasts, provided perfect madrigal texts, and Petrarch was Rore's favorite poet. However, the poem selected by Rore for the madrigal in this section is by an anonymous sixteenth-century poet.

After 1550 Italian poetry became increasingly pastoral in character, filled with shepherds and shepherdesses, nymphs, and similar allusions. Pastoral poems, or "pastorales," became the most important dramatic form in Italy and were often acted out. Whatever the poetic type, however, words and music were closely linked in the madrigals of Rore and became a prime consideration of the last group of Italian madrigalists, especially Marenzio and Gesualdo.

Performance

Madrigals were composed and performed for the purpose of providing entertainment for singers and, in the early period at least, were sung with one voice to each part. Like the chanson, the madrigal is essentially chamber music—intimate, subtle, and refined. Alec Harman and Anthony Milner, in their book *Man and His Music: Late Renaissance and Baroque Music*, have this to say concerning modern-day performance of madrigals: "Performances, alas too common today, in which each part is sung by six or more voices are as indefensible as playing a Mozart quartet on the strings of a symphony orchestra, for in doubling a vocal or instrumental part purity of intonation is lost, tone becomes rougher, and the gradations of nuance and expression coarsen" (p.23).

But some madrigals were meant to be doubled by voices or instruments. Those which were written for an outdoor performance needed to be reinforced since greater volume was needed.

The differences in the madrigals written by Arcadelt and those by Marenzio must be taken into consideration. In general, Arcadelt's madrigals and those of the first madrigal period should be performed with the speed of the half note or beat between M.M. 60 and 80. Those which are mainly chordal and rhythmically simple should be sung faster than those which are imitative and rhythmically complex. Once the tempo has been established, it should remain invariable. Rising and falling lines within an individual vocal phrase will naturally increase and decrease in volume, but there should be no powerful crescendos and diminuendos.

In the madrigals of Rore and Marenzio, the expressive range widens although one mood is generally felt throughout a single composition. Individual lines should be sung with a keen sense of the text, and in those in which word painting and mood change are dominant factors, more varied tempos and dynamics will be called for within the madrigal.

"Voi ve n'andat' al cielo"
("Now to the Heavens Are Turning")

I. **Title of Composition**
   "Voi ve n'andat' al cielo" ("Now to the Heavens Are Turning")

II. **Type of Composition**
   Italian madrigal

III. **Composer**
   Jacob Arcadelt (circa 1505-60), a Flemish composer, was one of the singers in the Papal Chapel in Rome from 1540 to 1549. He spent some time in Florence and then went to France where he was a member of the Chapel Royal in Paris. He composed three Masses, one book of motets, three Lamentations, and a volume of psalm settings. As a composer of secular music, Arcadelt was both prolific and renowned. He left some 250 Italian *frottole* and madrigals as well as numerous French chansons. Arcadelt is considered one of the most important composers in the early period of Italian madrigals.

IV. **Text**
   Both the Italian text and an English translation appear in the modern edition provided here for study and performance. The texts should be read by conductor and performers for clues concerning tempo and dynamics. The indications which appear in the music are editorial (there being none in the original) and merely serve as suggestions for performance.

V. **Background**
   Arcadelt's madrigals were published in large numbers during the 1530s and 1540s. "Now to the Heavens Are Turning" is representative of those published works. He found just the right musical techniques of chordal declamation or simple imitation to enhance the inflection of the text. The justification for Arcadelt's reputation as a suave melodist is clearly evident in this madrigal.

VI. **Structural and Stylistic Elements**

   A. **Medium**
      Soprano, alto, tenor, and bass.

   B. **Meter**
      This madrigal begins and ends in duple meter; a middle section is in triple meter.

C. **Rhythm**
Polyrhythmic sections, sections in which the individual voices move in different rhythms, are balanced with homorhythmic sections in which all the voices move in the same rhythm.

Examples
Polyrhythmic: mm. 1-25; 36-53; 57-58; 62-64.
Homorhythmic: mm. 26-35; 54-56; 59-61.

D. **Melody**
As in almost all Renaissance vocal music, conjunct or stepwise movement predominates in the melodies, with skips used to add variety or to emphasize the text. The melodic intervals used are major and minor seconds, major and minor thirds, perfect fourths, perfect fifths, minor sixths ascending, and octaves. The range of each individual line rarely exceeds an octave.

E. **Harmony**
The actual number of different harmonies used by Renaissance composers is relatively small. In this madrigal Arcadelt employed only major and minor triads in root position and first inversion. Although the diminished and augmented triads in first inversions were permitted, Arcadelt avoided them.

F. **Texture**
Basically homophonic with imitation used for variety.

G. **Text Setting**
Syllabic, one syllable to each note or chord.

H. **Form**
Through-composed with the last phrase repeated.

I. **Mode**
Ionian on A-flat.

VII. Additional Source
Arcadelt, Jacob. *Corpus mensurabilis musicae 31*. Edited by Albert Seay. Rome: American Institute of Musicology, 1948.

VIII. Recording
Jacob Arcadelt, Lyrichord Discs Inc., Stereo LLST-7199.

Now To The Heav'ns Are Turning

Voi ve n'andat'al cielo

Duration: 2 min., 40 sec.

SATB *a cappella*

Author unknown

English translation by Don Malin

JACQUES ARCADELT (*ca.*1505–*ca.* 1560)

edited by Don Malin

Note: The original note values have been halved and the pitch raised a minor third in this edition. However, it may be sung in the key of G if preferred. Also, all dynamic markings are the editor's.

15235–8

Example 5. "Now to the Heavens Are Turning." English translation and music editing by Don Malin. Copyright © 1968 Piedmont Music Company. International Copyright Secured. All Rights Reserved. Used by Permission.

4

15235—8

6

7

15235—8

8

S: they might gaze at me____ And be a - ware of my deep suf-
   hor ve-dre-ste poi____ Quel che dee' ha-ver un ben pie-to-

A: eyes, That they might gaze at me And be a - ware of my deep suf-
   voi, Ch'all hor ve - dre-ste poi Quel che dee' ha-ver un ben pie-to-

T: That they might gaze at me And be a - ware of my deep suf-
   Ch'all hor ve - dre-ste poi Quel che dee' ha-ver un ben pie-to-

B: they might gaze at me____ And be a - ware of my deep suf-
   hor ve-dre-ste poi____ Quel che dee' ha-ver un ben pie-to-

S: - fer - ing heart. And if you can not find me
   - so co - re. E se'l vo-stro ve - der voi

A: - f'ring____ heart. And if you can not____ find
   so co - re. E se'l vo-stro ve - der

T: - fer - ing heart. And if you can not
   - so co - re. E se'l vo-stro ve-

B: - fer - ing heart. And if you can not find me
   - so co - re. E se'l vo - stro ve-der voi

15235—8   *) These consecutive fifths in Soprano and Alto appear in the original.

10

"Da le belle contrade d'Oriente"
("From the Fair Realms of the East")

I. **Title of Composition**
   "Da le belle contrade d'Oriente" ("From the Fair Realms of the East")

II. **Type of Composition**
   Italian madrigal

III. **Composer**
   Cipriano de Rore (1516-65), a Netherlander, studied in Antwerp and Venice and worked in Ferrara and Parma. He succeeded his teacher, Adrian Willaert, as *maestro di cappella* at St. Mark's Cathedral in Venice. Rore is best known for his eight books of madrigals, the first of which, for five voices, appeared in 1542. He experimented with chromaticism and incorporated chromatic elements as part of the expressive technique of the madrigal. Rore also composed five Masses, three books of motets, a Passion, and a few instrumental works.

IV. **Text**
   The Italian text and an English translation appear in the modern edition provided here. The texts should be read by conductor and performers for clues concerning tempo and dynamics. The editor, Denis Stevens, offers suggestions for dynamics which should enhance the text.

V. **Background**
   This madrigal, based on a poem by an anonymous sixteenth-century Italian poet, exemplifies the skill, sensitivity, and originality with which Rore wedded music to text. Rore's madrigals were reprinted many times during his lifetime, and this Italian madrigal was probably used for study purposes since practical editions were published in separate partbooks. The existence of study scores attests to the esteem in which Rore was held by his contemporaries.

VI. **Structural and Stylistic Elements**

   A. **Medium**
      Soprano, alto, tenor 1 & 2, and bass.

   B. **Meter and Tempo**
      In this edition, the meter changes frequently to enhance the text: 6/4 to 4/4 to 8/4. The character of the poem and the polyphonic texture of the

51

music suggest that the half note or beat should be between M.M. 60-80.

C. Melody

Rore frequently used skips as well as chromaticism in melodic lines to express emotions suggested by the text. Even the bass part, which serves in a harmonic role, often approximates the melodic character of the other parts.

D. Texture

The texture is basically imitative with chordal segments. An important element in imitation is the amount of time which elapses between the successive voices. It is relatively rare in Renaissance music to find the entries spaced regularly, that is, voices entering regularly one or two measures apart. The irregularity of entries, called "staggered entrances," which appears in Rore's madrigal aids in keeping the rhythm of the composition "elastic" and helps to make each voice individual.

Notice the staggered entrance of voices in the first four measures of the composition: tenor 1 enters on the first beat of the first measure; the alto enters on the third beat of the first measure; the soprano and bass enter on the second beat of measure two; and tenor 2 enters on the second beat of measure four.

E. Accidentals and Cadences

It was customary in the Renaissance to end a piece with a major triad (or without any third in the chord at all) rather than with a minor triad, regardless of the mode in which the piece was written. This practice brought about the use of F sharp, C sharp, and G sharp. B flat had been in common usage in plainsong and can even be found in key signatures of polyphonic compositions during this period and before. Its use as an accidental brought about the introduction of E flat whenever a piece was transposed. These five accidentals, B flat, E flat, F sharp, C sharp, and G sharp, are the only ones which are found regularly in the music of the Renaissance. These chromatic notes helped to "color" the text and were used by the composer to express the text more fully.

VII. Additional Sources

Einstein, Alfred. *The Italian Madrigal*. Vol. 3. Princeton: Princeton University Press, 1949.

Rore, Cipriano de. *Corpus mensurabilis musicae 14*. Edited by Bernhard Meier. Vols. 3 and 4.   Rome: American Institute of Musicology, 1959.

VIII.Recording
Giovanni Gastoldi and Cipriano de Rore: Secular Vocal Music. The Musical Heritage Society, Inc. MHS 1930.

DA LE BELLE CONTRADE D'ORIENTE

Da le belle contrade d'oriente
Chiar' e lieta s'ergea Ciprigna, ed io
Fruiva in braccio as divini' idol mio
Quel piacer che non cape umana mente,

Quando senti dopp' un sospir ardente:
"Speranza del mio cor, dolce desio,
T'en vai, haimè, sola mi lasci! A dio!
Che sarà qui di me 'scura a dolente?

Ahi, crud' amor! Ben son dubbios' e corte
Le tue dolcezze, poich 'ancor ti godi
Che l'estremo piacer finisca in pianto!"

Ne potendo dir più, cinsemi forte,
Iterando gl'amplessi in tanti nodi,
Che giammai ne fer più l'edro o l'acanto.

From the fair realms of the East.
Brightly and cheerfully rose the dawn, and I
In the arms of my gorgeous goddess was enjoying
Such pleasure as eludes man's understanding

When I heard, after an ardent sigh:
"Hope of my heart, my sweet desire,
Thou goest, alas, thou leavest me alone! Farewell!
What will become of me here, in gloom and sadness?

Ah, cruel love! Uncertain indeed and brief
Are thy joys, since it even pleases thee
That the final pleasure should end in tears!"

Unable to say more, she hugged me close,
Repeating her embraces in so many coils
As never ivy did, or acanthus.

Notes on Performance

The dynamic level of the entire first section (through m. 31) should be relatively restrained, except for a warm glow at sunrise and an intensification of tone at appropriate points in the love scene. Make the most of the dramatic section (mm. 23-27) in which the disjointed texture calls for passionate sighs. The first forte should come at 32, with a mezzo-forte echo in the following measure; thereafter a gradual diminuendo so contrived that the closing section is mainly quiet, yet never devoid of expression. Strength and smoothness are the qualities to be brought out in the intertwining of ivy and acanthus, especially in the flowing melismata.

Denis Stevens

Example 6. Reprinted with permission.

DA LE BELLE CONTRADE D'ORIENTE

for SATTB Chorus A Cappella

Cipriano de Rore (1516-1565)
Il quinto Libro di Madrigali a cinque voci (Venice, 1566)
Edited by Denis Stevens

AB 1021

Printed in U.S.A.

4

6

8

AB 1021

"Già torna a rallegrar"
("Now Once More to All the Earth")

I. Title of Composition
"Già torna a rallegrar" ("Now Once More to All the Earth")

II. Type of Composition
Italian madrigal

III. Composer
Luca Marenzio (1553-99), an Italian composer and singer, was court musician for the Este family and for the king of Poland before he returned to Rome to serve the papal court. He composed in all the forms popular during his lifetime, writing numerous motets, court entertainments, sacred songs, and eighteen books of madrigals. Marenzio was one of those fortunate composers whose greatness was recognized during his lifetime and whose works were popular not only in Italy but throughout all of Europe. The beauty and skill of his writing caused him to be called *"il divino compositore"*—the divine composer.

IV. Text
Both the Italian text and an English translation appear in the music. It is suggested that both conductor and performers carefully read the texts since word painting is one of the most important characteristics of Marenzio's madrigals. Specific examples are cited under section VI, Structural and Stylistic Elements.

V. Background
Marenzio's fame as a madrigal composer largely rests on the madrigals he composed in his "first period," written before he was thirty. His more mature works were somewhat neglected. In his *A General History of Music*, the English music historian Charles Burney compared Marenzio's early and late compositions in the following excerpt:

> The first set of his madrigals for five voices, however, seems the most elaborate; the fugues and imitations here are more ingenious and frequent than in his other works. He has, indeed, in those of later date more melody; but as yet there was too little to compensate for the want of contrivance (v. 2, pp. 166-167, 1960 ed.).

The grace and skill of Marenzio's first period are summed up in the madrigal "Now Once More to All the Earth" in which the pastoral verse and diatonic vocal lines are pleasing both to sing and to hear.

VI. Structural and Stylistic Elements

A. **Medium**
Soprano I, soprano II, alto, tenor, and bass.

B. **Mode**
Ionian mode on G.

C. **Texture**
The texture is imitative with some chordal sections.

D. **Form**
Through-composed.

E. **Text**
Since Marenzio's most outstanding characteristic is word painting, the following sections should be examined:

1. mm. 1-9. *Rallegrar* is the Italian verb which means "to cheer or gladden." Marenzio treats this happy word with eighth notes which give the music a feeling of joyful movement.

2. mm. 14-21. Dancelike rhythms introduce fair April.

3. mm. 25-29. *Il mar* is the Italian for "the sea" which is represented by a wavy melodic line in all the voices.

4. mm. 30-31. *S'acqueta* is the Italian word for "quiet" or "calm." Voices sing in homorhythm, giving the music a feeling of "quiet" after the previous motion on the word *sea*.

5. mm. 32-39. *Sotterra* is the Italian word for "underground." Here Marenzio uses descending scale passages to express the feeling of frost melting into the ground.

6. mm. 56-72. After a joyful section telling of the happiness of Spring's sweet powers, a change of mood is felt in this section when the poet speaks of his weeping and sorrow. Marenzio portrays this mood with half notes which give the impression of a built-in retard and lessening of joy.

7. mm. 72 to end. Dancelike rhythms are used to express the happiness which will come when the sun unveils morrow.

VII. Additional Source

Marenzio, Luca. *The Secular Works.* Edited by Steven Ledbetter and Patricia Myers. New York: Broude Bros., 1977- .

2

Now Once More To All The Earth
(Già torna a rallegrar)

Duration: 2 min. 10 sec.

SSATB *a cappella*

English translation by
Don Malin

LUCA MARENZIO (1553–1599)
Edited by Don Malin

Observe these symbols throughout: **/** denoting an accented syllable, **∪** denoting an unaccented syllable.

Note: This edition is transposed a whole tone higher than the original. Also, all dynamic markings are the editor's.

15229–9

Example 7. "Now Once More to All the Earth." English translation and music editing by Don Malin. Copyright © 1968 Piedmont Music Company. International Copyright Secured. All Rights Reserved. Used by Permission.

4

15229-9

6

10

15229-9

"Il bell' humore"
("Good Humor")

I. Title of Composition
"Il bell' humore" ("Good Humor")

II. Type of Composition
Italian *balletto*

III. Composer
Giovanni Giacomo Gastoldi (circa 1550-1622) was born in Caravaggio (Lombardy) and at a very early age went to Mantua. It is believed that he studied there with the famous Flemish master, Giaches de Wert, whom he succeeded as choirmaster at Santa Barbara's. There he served under the Dukes Guglielmo and Vincenzo Gonzaga from 1582 to 1605. Gastoldi's secular works, of which the *balletti* are the most famous, are relatively few in number compared with his extensive sacred productions. From 1611 to his death in 1622, Gastoldi ceased to compose.

IV. Text
Both the Italian text and an English translation appear in the modern edition provided here. The texts should be read by conductor and performers for clues concerning tempo and dynamics. The indications which appear in the music are all editorial (there being none in the original) and merely serve as suggestions for performance.

V. Background
The book entitled *Balletti a cinque voci, per cantare, sonare, e ballare* (Balletti for five voices, to be sung, played, and danced) appeared as a fascinating novelty in the year 1591 when it was published in Venice. It reportedly became a best seller. The *balletti* are written for five parts, and each part bears a title representing a type of lover or a state of mind. As the title of the collection suggests, the *balletti* may be performed by voices and instruments in a variety of ways:

1. All parts may be sung *a cappella*.

2. All parts may be sung and doubled on instruments such as recorders and strings.

3. One of the soprano parts may be performed as a solo accompanied by lute or harpsichord.

4.   All parts may be played on instruments without vocal participation.

VI. **Structural and Stylistic Elements**

A.   **Medium**
Soprano I, soprano II, alto, tenor, and bass.

B.   **Meter and Tempo**
Duple; the tempo should be lively — allegro moderato.

C.   **Rhythm**
Mostly homorhythmic with some polyrhythms in the "fa-la" refrain.

D.   **Mode**
Ionian or major mode on G.

E.   **Form**
Strophic, same music for each of the two stanzas.

VII. **Additional Source**
Sanvoisin, Michael, ed. *Balletti a cinque voci 1591*. Paris: Heugel & Cie., 1968.

SIX BALLETTI

1. Il Bell' Humore

Good Humor

Viver lieto voglio
Senz'alcun cordoglio, La la la.
Tu puoi restar Amor
Di saettarmi il cor
Spendi i pungenti strali
Ove non paian frali
Nulla ti stimo o poco
E di te prendo gioco, La la la.

Senza alcun pensiero
Godo un piacer vero, La la la.
Ne puoi co'tuoi martir
Sturbar il mio gioir
Spegni pur la tua face
Che me non arde o sface
Nulla tem'io il tuo foco
E di te prendo gioco, La la la.

I want to live happily
Without any sorrow, La la la.
You can cease, Love,
To shoot arrows at my heart
Spend your piercing darts
That seem not fragile
I prize you little or naught
And I mock you, La la la.

Without any worry
I rejoice in true pleasure, La la la.
Nor can you with your tortures
Disturb my joy
Hide, too, your face
For it neither burns nor undoes me
I fear your fire not at all
And I mock you, La la la.

transl. by Gail Meadows

GIOVANNI GASTOLDI (c. 1550-1622)
ed. by H. C. Schmidt

Edition Peters 6877 a

4

do - glio, La la la   la la la   la la la   la la
ve - ro,

do - glio,   La la la   la la la   la la la
ve - ro,

do - glio,   La la   la la   la la la
ve - ro,

do - glio,   La la la   la la la   la la la la
ve - ro,

do - glio,   La la   la la   la la
ve - ro,

la la la   la.   la.
1. Tu   puoi res-tar A - mor   Di
2. Ne   puoi co'tuoi mar-tir   Stur-

la la la   la.   la.
1. Tu   puoi res-tar A -
2. Ne   puoi co'tuoi mar-

la la la   la.   la.
1. Tu   puoi res-tar A - mor   Di
2. Ne   puoi co'tuoi mar - tir   Stur-

la la la   la.   la.
1. Tu   puoi res-tar A -
2. Ne   puoi co'tuoi mar-

la la la   la.   la.
1. Tu   puoi res-tar A - mor   Di
2. Ne   puoi co'tuoi mar - tir   Stur-

6

The English Madrigal & Ballett

General Information

The form of the madrigal that developed in Italy during the sixteenth century became a prominent, popular form in England during the late Renaissance. In 1588, Nicholas Yonge, a singer at St. Paul's Cathedral in London, published *Musica transalpina* ("Music from Across the Alps"), a collection of Italian madrigals with English translations. This collection was immediately successful and helped to establish the madrigal-singing habit in England. Yonge, like many others, used his home as a place to gather "a great number of Gentlemen and Merchants of good accompt for the exercise of music daily" (Introduction, p.1). Soon madrigals were being sung in the parlors of great houses all over England, especially in those where families of refinement lived and entertained. The ability to read one's part at sight, when the partbooks were handed out after supper, was, according to Thomas Morley in his *A Plaine and Easie Introduction to Practicall Musicke*, "almost a necessary part of the equipment for social life" (p. 294). The influence of *Musica transalpina* caused the composition of English madrigals which often equalled their Italian models, and many balletts ("fa-la" songs) surpassed their models. Thus began the somewhat brief but brilliant period of the English madrigal.

One of the greatest English composers of the period, William Byrd (1543-1623), wrote excellent madrigals although he excelled in church music. His pupil Thomas Morley (1557-circa 1603) laid the foundation for the English school of madrigalists. Morley's madrigals have a tunefulness and sense of tonality greater than his Italian models. His strong feeling for dance rhythms introduced a popular element into the madrigal and set the fashion for most of his contemporaries. The dancelike features are most evident in length and polyphonic brilliance, especially in the "fa-la" refrains. Other leading composers of English madrigals and balletts were Thomas Weelkes (circa 1575-1623), and John Wilbye (1574-1628).

English Madrigal Texts

Most of the poems set to music by English madrigalists were of a pastoral or amatory nature and abound in classical allusions. While many were fanciful and high-flown, the poems of Edmund Spenser (circa 1552-99) and his followers, Sir Walter Raleigh (circa 1552-1618) and Sir Philip Sidney (1554-86) set a new standard for English madrigal verse. Regardless of the poem's literary merit, the setting of notes to words was always done with great skill. Mood changes are reflected in the music, and constant attention seems to be given to every expression of the poet, as far as possible. It seems that most English verse of the late Renaissance was written with a musical setting in mind.

Performance

Paintings of fifteenth- and sixteenth-century performers singing chansons and madrigals always show a very small group of soloists, not choirs. Madrigals, like other forms of secular music, were the vocal ensemble music of private gatherings and were therefore a form of chamber music. In most madrigals written after 1580, such as those by Weelkes, word painting and mood change are dominant factors. Sudden changes in dynamics and tempo are appropriate as are restrained diminuendos and crescendos. In general, the more varied the musical treatment of the text, the more varied the performance should be. The texts of many madrigals may suggest a range of effects from staccato to legato and from a light to a somber quality. Since vocal effects, tempo, and dynamics are largely determined by text, singers should first read the poem and decide together what is appropriate. Thomas Morley gave great insight into the performance practices of the English Renaissance. In *A Plaine and Easie Introduction to Practicall Musicke* he gave the following advice to madrigal performers:

> You must possesse your selfe with an amorus humor...so that you must in your musicke be wavering like the wind, sometime wanton, sometime drooping, sometime grave and staide, otherwhile effeminate...and the more varietie you shew the better shal you please (p. 294).

During the English Renaissance, madrigals were often performed instrumentally, or some verses would be sung and others played according to the available resources. English madrigals were often published with the instructions that they were "Apt for Voyces or Viols." In order to experience and hear fully the polyphony in the madrigal, try performing each one first with voices, then with instruments, and finally with both in combination.

The ballett should be sung lightly. The clear texture and dancelike rhythms call for a quick tempo of about M.M. 80 to 100 per halfnote. Although the expressive range is limited, variety can be achieved through dynamics and instrumental doubling of the vocal parts.

"I Thought that Love Had Been a Boy"

I. **Title of Composition**
   "I Thought that Love Had Been a Boy"

II. **Type of Composition**
   English madrigal

III. **Composer**
   William Byrd (circa 1540-1623), considered one of the greatest composers of the English Renaissance, was organist at Lincoln Cathedral in 1563 and Gentleman of the Chapel Royal in 1569. A composer of great versatility, he wrote church music for Roman and Anglican services, secular pieces such as madrigals and songs, and a wealth of keyboard music. Whether he wrote sacred or secular music, Byrd employed the imitative style with great dexterity and achieved expressive contrasts between homophony and polyphony. Byrd believed all vocal music should be "framed to the life of the words." In his collection of *Psalmes, Songs and Sonnets* he set down his famous reasons "to perswade every one to learne to sing" (p. 8). His recommendation ends with:

> Since singing is so good a thing
> I wish all men would learne to sing (p.8).

All his music subtly portrays the text.

IV. **Text**
   The text should be read by conductor and performers for clues concerning tempo and dynamics. Such indications which appear in the music are all editorial (there being none in the original) and merely serve as suggestions for performance.

V. **Background**
   Byrd's madrigals were among the earliest such pieces written in England. They are almost art songs and, as the late English musicologist Edmund Fellowes explained in his *The English Madrigal Composers*, "to be performed alternatively, either by combined voices or by solo voice and accompanied by strings" (pp. 77-78). The main voice (referred to by Byrd as "the first part") presented a continuous melodic line, in place of a repetition of phrases to which later madrigalists were partial. The other voices, or viols, served as accompaniment. Byrd's madrigal texts were usually of a contemplative or somber nature. "I Though that Love Had Been A Boy" is one that shows the light, lyrical setting of the poem. It should be noted that

in classical mythology "love" was portrayed as a boy, often blindfolded, who followed after Venus, the ancient Italian goddess of gardens and spring. The phrase "love is blind" descends from this idea as well as the visual image of Cupid.

VI. **Structural and Stylistic Elements**

    A. **Medium**
    Soprano I, soprano II, alto, tenor, and bass.

    B. **Texture**
    Basically homophonic.

    C. **Mode**
    Ionian mode on F.

    D. **Harmonies**
    The actual number of harmonies used in Renaissance music is small. Basically they are (1) major and minor triads in root position, (2) major and minor triads in their first inversions, and (3) the diminished triad in first inversion and occasionally in root position. In the opening of Byrd's madrigal, all triads are in root position:

Example 9. Byrd, "I Though that Love Had Been a Boy," mm. 1-6.

    E. **Cadences**
    The final cadences used in Renaissance music are of four types: *perfect authentic*, *imperfect*, *Phrygian*, and *plagal*. The *perfect authentic* consists of a progression from a major dominant triad to a major triad built on the final. This type of cadence is common to all modes *except* the *Phrygian*. The *perfect* cadence requires a chromatic raising of the third both in the last chord and in the one which precedes it, in case they are not already major. It should be noted that the final chord may be either complete or incomplete. Sometimes the third is omitted, and sometimes the fifth is

omitted. In any case, both chords are in root position. An *imperfect* cadence is the same except the tonic chord is in another arrangement, that is, with the third or the fifth in the soprano. Byrd ends this piece with an *imperfect* cadence.

Example 10. Byrd, "I Though that Love Had Been a Boy," p.6, mm. 41-46.

F.   Form
      Through-composed.

VII. Additional Source
Fellowes, Edmund, ed. *The English Madrigal School*. Vol. 15. London: Stainer and Bell, Ltd., 1923.

VIII. Recording
William Byrd, Lyrichord Discs, LLST-7156.

I thought that Love had been a boy

Five-part Madrigal for Mixed Voices
(a cappella)

Of unknown authorship

Edited, and the accompaniment
arranged, by H. Clough-Leighter

William Byrd
(1543-1623)

Example 11. © Copyright 1933 (renewed 1960) by E. C. Schirmer Music Company.

4

"Sing We and Chant It"

I. **Title of Composition**
"Sing We and Chant It"

II. **Type of Composition**
English ballett

III. **Composer**
Thomas Morley (1557- circa 1603) was one of England's most famous organists and composers. He was a pupil of William Byrd's and also studied at Oxford where he received the bachelor of music degree in 1588. After leaving his post as organist at St. Paul's Cathedral, he entered the Chapel Royal in 1592. Morley was a leader of the English madrigal school and enjoyed great success during his lifetime. His devotion to the Italian *balletto* form, with its "fa-la" refrains, accounts for much of his popularity, both in his own time and today. Morley's book, *A Plaine and Easie Introduction to Practicall Musicke*, which was written in dialogue form between master and pupil, is a valuable treatise on modal music and the performance practices of his time. Besides composing balletts, Morley wrote madrigals and lute songs. He is also known for having furnished music for the first performance of some of Shakespeare's plays, including *As You Like It*.

IV. **Text**
The text should be read by conductor and performers for clues concerning tempo and dynamics. The indications which appear in the music are all editorial (there being none in the original) and merely serve as suggestions for performance.

V. **Background**
The *balletto*, a popular Italian form, was introduced into England by Thomas Morley in *The First Book of Balletts for Five Voices* which was published in 1595. Morley was one of England's most significant creators of this form.

VI. **Structural and Stylistic Elements**

A. **Medium**
Soprano I, soprano II, alto, tenor, and bass.

B. **Meter and Melody**
Triple meter; the melody is felt in four-bar phrases except for the ending which is in three-bar phrases, that is, the last three measures of each complete strophe.

C.   **Mode**
Mixolydian, but with strong tonic-dominant chords which give the effect of major.

D.   **Texture**
The verses tend to be homophonic, and the "fa-la" refrains are polyphonic.

E.   **Dissonances**
Two of the most typical dissonances or non-harmonic tones used by sixteenth-century composers appear in this madrigal. They are called (1) passing tone and (2) suspension.

   1.   Passing tone
        a)   *Usually* moves on weak part of beat.
        b)   *Always* ascends or descends stepwise from one consonance to another.
        c)   *Always* continues in the direction by which it is approached.

        Examples
        m. 3 Double passing tones in soprano I and II on the word *love*.
        m. 3 Passing tone on the last half beat in alto on c'.

   2.   Suspension

        A dissonance found on *accented* part of the measure. Suspensions involve three specific steps:

        a)   Preparation—*Always* on unaccented beat.
        b)   Suspension—*Always* on the following accented beat.
        c)   Resolution—*Always* on the following unaccented beat.

        P-S-R refers to the movement of a single voice part.

        Example
        mm. 6 & 7. Suspension in soprano II.

F.   **Cadences**
Examples
mm. 7-8. V-I or imperfect cadence ends this and all other sections; imperfect because third, rather than tonic, is in the soprano.

G.   Form
Strophic, the same music is used for each stanza.

VII. Additional Source
Fellowes, Edmund, ed. *The English Madrigal School*. Vol. 4. London: Stainer and Bell, Ltd., 1923.

VIII.Recording
Elizabethan Madrigals, Canzonettes and Ballets. The Primavera Singers. Noah Greenberg, cond. Esoteric Records, No. 5520, 1313 N. Vine Street, Hollywood 28, California.

Sing we and chant it

Five-part Ballet for Mixed Voices
(a cappella)

Attributed to
Michael Drayton
(1563 - 1631)

Thomas Morley
(1557 - 1603)

Edited by H. Clough-Leighter

Published, 1932, by E. C. Schirmer Music Co.
Boston, Mass

Example 12. Reprinted from the *A Cappella Singer*, © Copyright 1936 (renewed 1964)
by E. C. Schirmer Music Company.

The German Lied

General Information

The Lied (leet) is a song in the German language. In Germany, monophonic Lieder (leed-er, "songs") were composed as early as the twelfth century and as late as the sixteenth century during the Minnesinger and Meistersinger movements. Although polyphonic Lieder existed in the fifteenth century, the finest examples in the early sixteenth century were composed by the Netherlander Heinrich Isaac (eez'-ahk) (circa 1450-1517). Isaac employed the full range of stylistic elements in his polyphonic songs: simple chord-like settings, songs with a borrowed melody placed in the tenor, and freely composed compositions in imitative style. Toward the middle of the sixteenth century a new style of Lieder began to emerge. The Lieder of Isaac's pupil Ludwig Senfl (ZEN-ful) (circa 1488-1543) show a complete mastery of polyphonic technique with graceful and expressive melodies in all voices, not only the tenor. The Lieder composed during the later sixteenth century show the influence of the Italian madrigal which was popular in Germany at that time. The songs of the German composer Hans Leo Hassler (1564-1612), who studied with Andrea Gabrieli in Venice, show strong Italian characteristics and are among the best of the entire Renaissance.

Texts

Lieder texts came from many different sources and covered a wide variety of subjects. Many texts dealt with subjects such as drinking, hunting, war, and politics. Lieder texts written for the court were more aristocratic in style and extolled loyalty, good breeding, and manners. Many Lieder texts dealt with love and were sentimental expressions of grief at the departure of a loved one or at the faithlessness of a lover.

Performance

Instrumental participation in vocal music was much more common in Germany than in other countries during the Renaissance due to Germany's strong instrumental tradition. Lieder need not be sung; they can just as well be performed on a single instrument such as a lute, harpsichord, or organ. The most important voice part, which is the tenor in early sixteenth-century Lieder and the treble in late sixteenth-century Lieder, can be sung as solo accompanied by an instrument or group of instruments such as strings and woodwinds, especially recorders. Lieder in the sixteenth century were often performed entirely on instruments. Instruments can be grouped in a homogeneous ("whole") consort or in a heterogeneous ("broken") consort. While a combination of voices and instruments adds variety and interest to German secular songs, it should be pointed out that Lieder can be performed unaccompanied with one or two singers to a part. The beat of the half note will be between M.M. 60 to 90.

"Innsbruck, ich muss dich lassen" ("Innsbruck, I Now Must Leave Thee")

I. Title of Composition
"Innsbruck, ich muss dich lassen" ("Innsbruck, I Now Must Leave Thee")

II. Type of Composition
German Lied

III. Composer
Heinrich Isaac (circa 1450-1517), a Netherlander, enjoyed an international career. He is first heard of in 1485, at Innsbruck, when he was on his initial trip to Italy. While there he worked for Lorenzo the Magnificent in Florence and for the Duke of Ferrara. Isaac later became the court composer to Emperor Maximilian I at Vienna and Innsbruck. His association with Maximilian's chapel lasted until 1515. Isaac then returned to Florence, dying there in 1517. He was a prolific composer who wrote numerous Masses, motets, and psalm settings. He is renowned for his *Choralis Constantinus*, a large collection of Mass Propers and motets for the entire church year. Isaac also wrote some eighty secular songs with French, Italian, and German texts. His German songs have proven to be not only the most numerous of his secular compositions but the most popular as well.

IV. Text
Both the German text and an English translation appear in the modern edition provided here for study and performance. The texts should be read by conductor and performers for clues concerning tempo and dynamics. Such indications which appear in the music are all editorial (there being none in the original) and merely serve as suggestions for performance.

V. Background
This composition is one of the most beautiful of the Renaissance. The text, ascribed to Maximilian I of Austria, expresses nostalgia for the lovely city of Innsbruck. The melody, which may not have been written by Isaac, was adapted to sacred words and became widely known as "O world, I now must leave thee." The practice of adding new words to a preexistent melody is known as *contrafactum* and the practice of writing *contrafacta* was already a common one in the Middle Ages. The beautiful "Innsbruck" melody was later harmonized by J. S. Bach, and used as a chorale in his *St. Matthew Passion*.

VI. Structural Elements

A. Medium
Soprano, alto, tenor, and bass.

B. Meter
The music alternates between triple and duple meter throughout.

C. Rhythm
Basically homorhythmic; all voices move in the same rhythm except for slight variations in one or two voices.

D. Melody
The main melody is in the top voice, or superius.

E. Texture
Homophonic or chordal.

F. Mode
Ionian or major mode on G.

G. Dissonance
Three of the most common nonharmonic tones or dissonances found in "Innsbruck, ich muss dich lassen" are (1) suspensions, (2) double passing tones, and (3) anticipations.

1. Suspensions
   A dissonance found on the *accented* part of the beat. Suspensions have three specific steps:

   a) Preparation: *Always* on unaccented beat.
   b) Suspension: *Always* on accented beat.
   c) Resolution: *Always* on the following unaccented beat.

   P-S-R refers to the movement of a single voice part.

   Example
   mm. 2 and 3   Suspension in the alto.

Example 13. Isaac, "Innsbruck, ich muss dich lassen," p. 3, mm. 1-3.

2.   Passing tone
      Usually moves on weak part of beat.
      Always ascends or descends stepwise from one consonance to anoth-
      er.
      Always continues in the direction by which it is approached.

      Example
      double passing tones
      m. 15   b' in soprano and f' sharp in alto.

Example 14. Isaac, "Innsbruck, ich muss dich lassen," p. 5, mm. 15-18.

3.   Anticipation
      The sounding of a note before the chord to which it belongs.

      Example
      m. 16   g' in soprano.

Example 15. Isaac, "Innsbruck, ich muss dich lassen," p. 5, mm. 15-18.

H. Form
Through-composed.

VII. Additional Sources

Adler, Guido, gen. ed. *Denkmäler der Tonkunst in Österreich*. Vienna: Artaria and Company, 1894.

Isaac, Heinrich. *Weltliche Werke*. Edited by J. Wolf. 2nd ed. Graz: Akademische Druck-u. Verlagsanstalt, 1959.

VIII. Recording

Secular Music of the Renaissance. The Musical Heritage Society, Inc. MHS 713. 1991 Broadway, New York, NY, 10023.

Duration ca. 1'35"

Innsbruck, ich muss dich lassen

Innsbruck, I Now Must Leave Thee

O World, I Now Must Leave Thee

for Four-Part Chorus of Mixed Voices a cappella**

Secular German text: Archduke Max(?), 1495
English version by K.S.
Sacred English text (based on an anonymous
German text of ca. 1555) by K.S. *

Heinrich Isaac
(ca. 1450-1517)
Edited by Kurt Stone

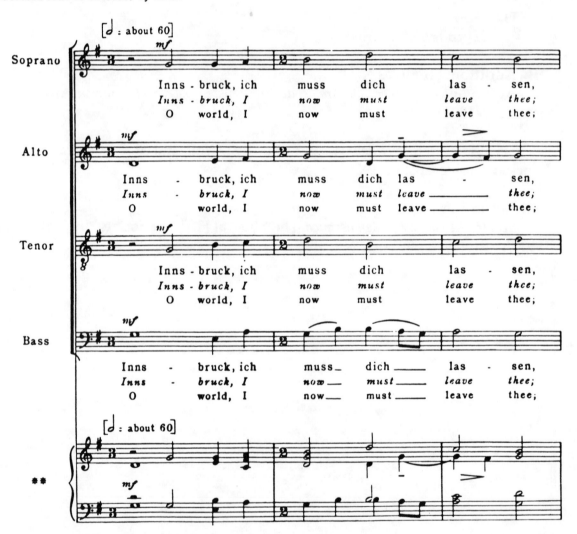

\# used by permission
\#\# see Introductory Note

Example 16. Reprinted with permission.

"Wohlauf, jung und alt"
("Arise, Young and Old")

I. **Title of Composition**

"Wohlauf, jung und alt" ("Arise, Young and Old")

II. **Type of Composition**

German Lied

III. **Composer**

Ludwig Senfl (c. 1492-c. 1543), a pupil of the Netherland composer Heinrich Isaac, is considered the Swiss master of Renaissance polyphony. He was Isaac's successor at the Imperial Court in Vienna, working there for Maximilian I of Austria. Senfl also held posts at the courts in Brandenburg and Munich. He held the position of court *Kapellmeister* in Munich until his death in 1543. Senfl composed both sacred and secular works, including Masses, motets, and German Lieder. His Lieder were so popular that they led to his being called "the prince of German music."

IV. **Text and Translations**

The German text and English translation appear in the modern edition provided here. The text should be read by conductor and performers for clues concerning tempo and dynamics. Notice Senfl's creative use of text painting, mm. 44-48, as the fearless dogs "woof" when they give chase to the stag.

V. **Background**

This Lied by Senfl is characteristic of the polyphonic/homophonic (hybrid texture) song popular in Germany during the first half of the sixteenth century. The German Lied was one of the distinct national secular forms of the Renaissance, comparable to the chanson in France and the madrigal in Italy and England. In most Lieder, a German folk song is used as a *cantus firmus*, or fixed song, to which other voices are added by the composer. This Lied by Senfl is an exception, the *cantus firmus* being a number of different songs appearing in the tenor one after the other. Therefore, this piece is known as a *quodlibet*, a composition in which two or more melodies are contrapuntally combined.

VI. **Structural and Stylistic Elements**

A. **Medium**

Soprano, alto, tenor, and bass.

B.   **Meter**
Triple and duple.

C.   **Melody**
Several German folk tunes, used as a *cantus firmus*, appear in the tenor.
Around these melodies Senfl weaves other motives which are derived
from phrases of the tunes.

D.   **Texture**
Hybrid; both homophonic and polyphonic textures.

E.   **Mode**
Ionian mode on C.

F.   **Form**
Through-composed.

VII. Additional Source
Senfl, Ludwig. *Sämtliche Werke.* Wolfenbüttel: Möseler, 1949 - .

VIII.Recording
Ludwig Senfl. *Deutsche Lieder: Swiss Composers.* CT-64-3.

2

Arise, Young and Old
Wohlauf, Jung und Alt
for Four-Part Chorus of Mixed Voices a cappella

Duration about 1:30 minutes

Anonymous
English version by
C. G. R. and Kurt Stone

Ludwig Senfl (1492?-1555)
Edited by Clifford G. Richter

Example 17. Reprinted with permission.

4

6

"Ach Schatz Ich Thu Dir Klagen"
("Oh Love, Hear Thou My Pleading")

I.   Title of Composition
"Ach Schatz Ich Thu Dir Klagen " ("Oh Love, Hear Thou My Pleading")

II.   Type of Composition
German Lied

III.   Composer
Hans Leo Hassler (1564-1612), great German organist and composer, was born in Nuremberg. In 1584 he left Germany to study with Andrea Gabrieli in Venice. From 1585 until his death he held various positions at Augsburg, Nuremberg, Ulm, and finally at Dresden, where he was organist for the Elector of Saxony. His many and various compositions include Latin Masses and motets, German Lieder, settings of Lutheran chorales, canzonets and madrigals with Italian texts, organ works, and instrumental pieces in the form of intradas and canzonas. Donald Grout states in *A History of Western Music* that Hassler achieved in his music "a fruitful union of Italian sweetness with German seriousness" (p. 276). Besides being the greatest German composer of the late sixteenth century, Hassler was also a metal dealer and a maker of musical clocks.

IV.   Text
Both the German text and an English translation appear in the modern edition provided here. The texts should be read by conductor and performers for clues concerning tempo and dynamics. The indications which appear in the music are all editorial (there being none in the original) and merely serve as suggestions for performance.

V.   Background
As a composer of Lieder, Hassler stands in direct line of succession to Isaac and Senfl. In Hassler's Lieder, however, Italian and German qualities are often synthesized. The beautiful Lied "Ach Schatz" first appeared in 1596 in a collection entitled *Neue teutsche Gesäng nach art der selschen Madrigalien und Canzonetten*, which contained twenty-four pieces for four to eight voices. These Lieder are more simply constructed than Hassler's Italian madrigals and show a depth of expression which is essentially German.

VI. Structural and Stylistic Elements

A. Medium
Soprano I, soprano II, alto, tenor, and bass.

B. Meter and Tempo
Duple. The editorial suggestion of an *Andante* tempo is in keeping with the sentiment of the composition.

C. Texture
Homophonic or chordal.

D. Form
AABB; the second B section begins in the middle of m. 36.

VII. Additional Source

Hassler, Hans Leo. *Sämtliche Werke*. Vol. 2. *Canzonette von 1590 und Neue Teutsche Gesäng von 1596*. Edited by Rudolf Schwartz. Wiesbaden: Breitkopf und Härtel, 1961.

VIII. Recording

Historical Anthology of Music, Late Sixteenth-Century Music, Part 2, Pleiades Records, P256.

Example 18. "Oh Love, Hear Thou My Pleading" ("Ach Schatz Ich Thu Dir Klagen"), Hans Hassler, © 1970 WB Music Corp. All Rights Reserved. Used by Permission.

4

6

8

The Renaissance Motet

General Information

The motet (mo-TET) constituted a large portion of Catholic church music composed during the Renaissance and was important as a musical form second only to the Mass. The motet began in France around 1200 but underwent such numerous changes of style that it is impossible to formulate a general definition which covers all phases of its development. By 1500 in the influential Flemish school, however, it had become a sacred choral composition based on a Latin text and designed to be performed in the Proper of the Mass and during certain hours, mainly vespers, a service performed at sunset. The classical Flemish "motet style" of Josquin Desprez (zhoss-can day pray) is characterized by imitation and by alternating polyphonic and homophonic textures. After 1550 the motet spread throughout Europe and became a favorite form of such leading Renaissance composers as Palestrina in Italy, Victoria in Spain and Italy, William Byrd in England, and Orlando di Lasso and Hans Leo Hassler in Germany.

Motet Texts

Renaissance composers chose motet texts from a variety of sources with the majority taken from the Scriptures, mainly psalms. The wide range of texts offered composers more interesting possibilities for word-music relationships than did the invariable texts of the Mass. Josquin Desprez took great care to suit music to text and to give strong and detailed reflections to the words of his motets, a practice known in the sixteenth century as *musica reservata*, literally "reserved music." The fact that motets gave composers the opportunity to be more musically expressive made it, rather than the Mass, the favored form of sacred composition during the sixteenth century.

Performance

Unlike the secular music of the sixteenth century which was performed with one singer to a part, the minimum number of singers required for sacred music is generally twelve to twenty-four. Thurston Dart, author of *The Interpretation of Music*, states that to decide the maximum number of singers is more difficult since the size of a choir was probably governed by the amount of money the owner could afford to spend on keeping it up. From several accounts we learn that the size of choirs was not standardized in the Renaissance any more than it is today. Choirs ranged from eight to the sixty-one singers used by Orlando di Lasso in the royal court of Bavaria in Munich. It is known that the Papal Choir in Rome had ten singers in 1442 but by 1483 the number had increased to twenty-four and more or less remained at that number throughout the sixteenth century. Motets can be varied at suitable places by altering both the number and combination of voices. Instruments, such as organs, viols, and recorders may be used to double the voices. The tempo should be governed by the words, but generally the speed of the tactus or beat is between M.M. 60-80. Dynamic contrasts are indeed suitable in the expressive form of the motet but should be restrained and never extreme.

Women's voices were not used to perform sacred music in the Renaissance. The soprano and alto parts were sung by boys, countertenors, or men singing falsetto. Therefore women singing Renaissance motets and Masses today should always strive for as clear and light a voice quality as possible.

2. "Ave Maria, Gratia Plena"
("Hail Mary, Full of Grace")

I.   Title of Composition
2. "Ave Maria, Gratia Plena" ("Hail Mary, Full of Grace")

II.   Type of Composition
Renaissance motet

III.   Composer
Josquin Desprez was probably born in Picardy, that part of the lowlands which today lies on the Franco-Belgian border, in the year 1450. He began his musical career as a choirboy and later became one of the most learned and influential musicians of his time. He traveled to Italy where he was employed by the Sforzas in Milan, the Papal Chapel in Rome, and the Duke of Ferrara. After the duke's death in 1505, Josquin returned to his homeland where he died in 1521. His compositions include some seventy chansons, twenty-two Masses, numerous motets, hymns, and psalm settings. The beauty and skill found in his music caused him even in his day to be called the "Father of Musicians."

IV.   Text
The text is a well-known poem of the Middle Ages which commemorates the major events in the life of the Virgin Mary. A translation appears in the introductory remarks to the music. Both the Latin text and the English translation should be read by conductor and performers for clues concerning tempo and dynamics. The indications which appear in the music are all editorial (there being none in the original) and merely serve as suggestions for performance.

V.   Background
Although Josquin's genius as a composer is evident in all his compositions, it was in the motets that he made his most creative contribution. The motet presented here is a masterpiece of the middle Renaissance (circa 1500-1525) and an excellent example of Josquin's motet style.

VI.   Structural and Stylistic Elements

   #### A.   Medium
   Soprano, alto, tenor, and bass.

   #### B.   Meter
   Duple, except for a short middle section in triple meter in mm. 94-108.

C. **Rhythm**
Polyrhythmic sections, sections in which the individual voices move in different rhythms, are the norm for this motet except for two short sections in homorhythm, sections in which the voices move in the same rhythm. Such sections were often referred to as passages in "familiar style."

Examples
Homorhythmic sections: mm. 94-109 and m. 143 to the end of the piece.

D. **Texture**
Except for the two homophonic-homorhythmic sections mentioned above, the texture for this motet is imitative counterpoint, that is, the use of the same thematic material in all the parts. The opening section is a perfect example of "real" imitation so evident in motets before 1550 in which each voice enters in an exact transposition of the first voice, or subject.

E. **Voice Pairing**
Josquin often varied the texture of his compositions by pairing the voices so that soprano and alto are answered by tenor and bass, or in similar combinations.

Examples
mm. 31-39   Soprano and alto are answered by tenor and bass.
mm. 78-93   Soprano and alto are answered by tenor and bass twice.

F. **Use of Canon**
The use of canon was as natural a form of expression to Josquin as the fugue was to Bach. A canon is employed at the fifth below between soprano and tenor at mm. 94-109. The tenor follows one beat after the soprano, and the alto and bass are free.

G. **Mode**
Ionian.

H. **Dissonances**
Three of the most common dissonances, or nonharmonic tones, found in "Ave Maria, Gratia Plena" are 1) passing tones, 2) suspensions, and 3) anticipations.

1. Passing tone
Usually moves on weak part of beat.

Always ascends or descends stepwise from one consonance to another.

Always continues in the direction by which it is approached.

Examples
m. 8   Passing tone b′ in soprano.
m. 12   Passing tone b in tenor.

2.   Suspensions
A dissonance found on *accented* part of the beat. Suspensions have three specific steps:

a)   Preparation: *always* on unaccented beat.
b)   Suspension: *always* on the following accented beat.
c)   Resolution: *always* on the following unaccented beat.

P-S-R refers to the movement of a single voice part.

Example
mm. 23-24:   g′ in tenor is preparation note.
             g′ in tenor is suspension.
             f′ sharp in tenor is resolution.

3.   Anticipation
The sounding of a note or notes before the chord to which it or they belong.

Example
m. 38   Double anticipation, b in alto and e′ in tenor.

I.   Cadences
Josquin achieves continuity by the device of overlapping cadences; before one phrase ends in all voices, one voice will begin a new phrase. Seldom do all voices cadence at the same time.

Example
m. 16   The soprano begins the third phrase on the word *Dominus* while the tenor and bass complete the second phrase on *gratia plena*.

VII. Additional Source
Des Prez, Josquin. *Werke*. Edited by Albert Smijers. Leipzig: Kistner und Siegel, 1925.

VIII.Recording
Anthology of Renaissance Music. Dover 95248-7.

Text: Ave Maria

Hail Mary, full of grace, the Lord is with thee, joyous Virgin. Hail thee whose conceiving, full of solemn gladness, fills heaven and earth with a new joy. Hail thee whose birth was to us a holy day, o thou who surpassest the shining light in the east, the very sun. Hail thy humanity, thy conception without a man, thou whose annunciation was our salvation. Hail thy true virginity, thy spotless chastity, thou whose purification was our expiation. Hail thee, most excellent in all angelic goodness, thou whose assumption was our glorification. O Mother of God, remember me. Amen.

Translated by William Earle Nettles
Research Associate
New York Pro Musica

Example 19. "Ave Maria, Gratia Plena (SATB)" by Josquin Desprez. Copyright 1969 by Associated Music Publishers (BMI). International copyright secured. All rights reserved.

Duration: ca. 4 minutes

Two Marian Motets
for Four-Part Chorus of Mixed Voices, a cappella

Josquin Desprez
(ca. 1450-1521)

Edited by Noah Greenberg

2. Ave Maria, Gratia Plena

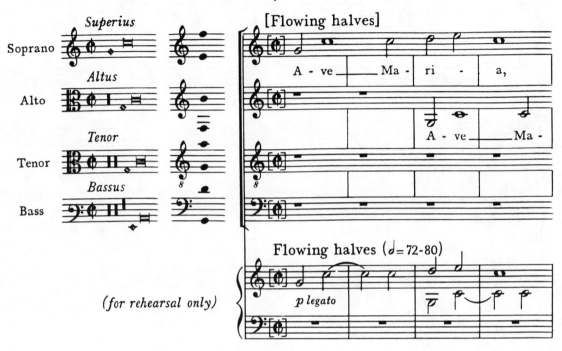

(for rehearsal only)

Printed in U.S.A.

4

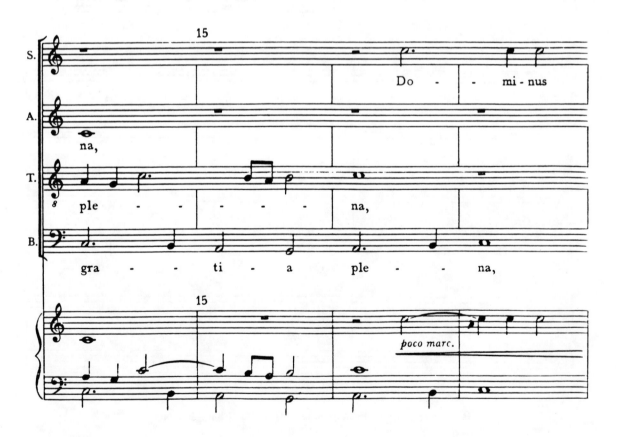

6

8

12

14

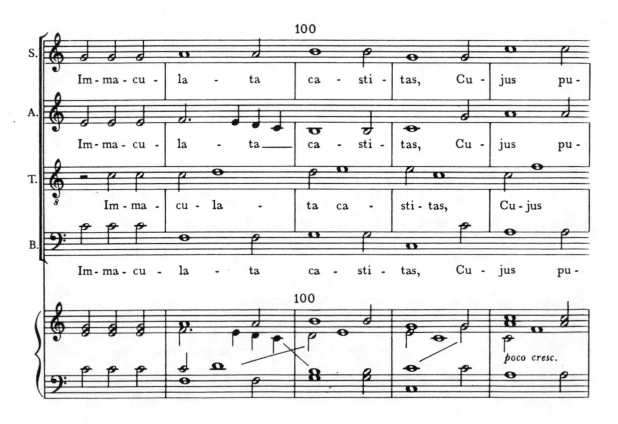

16

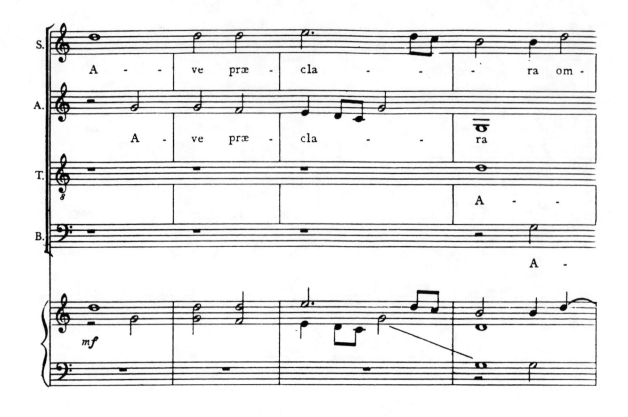

20

The Mass

General Information

The Mass constitutes the main service of the Roman Catholic Church, representing the commemoration and mystical reenactment of the sacrifice of Christ on the cross. The name is derived from the words "Ite, missa est [congregation]" which are sung at the end of the service and which mean "Depart, the congregation is dismissed." The Mass falls into two parts: the Proper, the texts of which vary from day to day; and the Ordinary, the texts of which are invariable. For over fifteen hundred years, parts of the Mass have been set to music. During the Renaissance, however, composers of polyphonic music usually set the five items of the Ordinary. These are:

> Kyrie Eleison (Lord, have mercy)
> Gloria in Excelsis (Glory be to God on high)
> Credo (I believe in One God)
> Sanctus (Holy, Holy, Holy)
> Agnus Dei (Lamb of God)

Several types of Mass composition were employed by Renaissance composers. One popular type was the so-called Parody Mass in which all or some of a previously composed piece (madrigal, motet, chanson) was borrowed and reworked to accommodate the text of each Mass movement. In this type the composer often alternated borrowed material with sections of newly composed material. Another type almost as common as the parody technique was the *cantus firmus* (fixed song) Mass. In this type the composer selected a sacred or secular tune around which he wove new material, and all the movements were based on the same tune. Not all Masses were based on previously composed material, however, and in freely invented Masses the composer wrote all his own material.

One type of Mass popular during the Renaissance was the *Missa brevis* (short Mass) which took less time to perform than a regular Mass due to its simpler, more homophonic style and syllabic text setting. This type was generally favored during the Counter Reformation because of its simplicity.

Texts

The Kyrie text, which is in Greek rather than Latin, consists of three invocations: "Kyrie eleison," "Christe eleison," "Kyrie eleison" (God have mercy, Christ have mercy, God have mercy). Each invocation is sung three times. The Agnus Dei also consists of three invocations: "Agnus Dei, qui tollis peccata mundi, miserere

147

nobis," "Agnus Dei . . . miserere nobis," "Agnus Dei . . . dona nobis pacem" (Lamb of God, who takest away the sins of the world, have mercy upon us, Lamb of God . . . have mercy upon us, Lamb of God . . . grant us Thy peace.)

Performance

Renaissance Masses, particularly those of Palestrina, should be performed in a restrained manner. Alec Harman, author of *Man and His Music: Mediaeval and Early Renaissance Music,* gives the following performance suggestions for the Ordinary of the Mass based on statements by the sixteenth-century Italian theorist Franchino Gafori:

> The speed of the tactus, within the limits of M.M. 60-80, should be governed by the nature of the words and/or the texture of the music . . . . In the mass the Kyrie, Sanctus and Agnus Dei, because they need more time to fully display their flowing melismatic lines and rich polyphonic texture, should be slower than the Gloria and Credo, in which the number of words is far greater and hence the melodies are more syllabic and the texture less complex. There should, however, be slight differences in speed within the Gloria (e.g., "Qui tollis"—either the first or second statement, depending on how the composer has sectionalized the music— to "suscipe deprecationem nostram" inclusive should be slower), the Credo (e.g., "Crucifixus" to "sepultus est" should be slower), and the Sanctus (e.g., "Pleni sunt coeli et terra gloria tua" should be quicker and the "Osanna" quicker still, i.e., "Sanctus . . ." could be M.M. 60, "Pleni sunt coeli . . ." M.M. 70, and "Osanna . . ." M.M. 80) (p. 229).

Harman goes on to say that once the speed of the tactus has been set for a complete work or section it should remain unchanged. Nothing does greater violence to Renaissance music than constantly fluctuating tempos and excessive accelerandos and rallentandos. This, of course, is more the case with sacred music than with secular music of the period. Suggestions concerning number of singers, dynamics, and other performance practices were discussed in the section dealing with the Renaissance motet and are applicable to the performance of the Mass as well.

"Kyrie" from *Missa Brevis*

I. Title of Composition
"Kyrie" from *Missa Brevis*

II. Type of Composition
Mass movement

III. Composer
Giovanni Pierluigi da Palestrina (circa 1526-94) was an Italian composer of the late Renaissance who maintained a purity of style and a mastery of contrapuntal structure throughout his composing career. He began his musical study as a choirboy at Santa Maria Maggiore in Rome. In 1544 he became musical director at the cathedral in Palestrina, whose bishop became Pope Julius III. The pope brought Palestrina to Rome where the new decrees on simplifying sacred music found fruition in the composer's forthright style. Palestrina composed over 100 Masses, some 450 motets, 42 psalm settings, various Magnificats, litanies, and Lamentations, as well as some 200 sacred and secular madrigals.

IV. Text
Both the Greek text and English translation appear under Texts in the introductory information for the Renaissance Mass.

V. Background
The *Missa Brevis*, which appears in Palestrina's third book of Masses (1570), is one of the simplest of his compositions, as well as one of the most beautiful. This Mass may be based on a theme from *Audi filia*, a Mass by the French composer, Claude Goudimel (1510-72). However, Palestrina most likely derived some or all of the melodies from Gregorian chant sources.

VI. Structural and Stylistic Elements

A. Medium
Soprano, alto, tenor, and bass.

B. Meter
Duple.

C. Melody
Palestrina, like most Renaissance composers, restricted the range of his

149

melodies. The melodies which appear in this Kyrie are restricted to a few notes which no doubt show the influence of plainchant. The melodic intervals used are the same as those found in plainchant, that is, major and minor seconds, major and minor thirds, perfect fourths, perfect fifths, and perfect octaves. All these intervals are used ascending and descending. The minor sixth, however, is only used ascending. Rarely are chromatic, augmented, or diminished intervals used in this strict style of composition. Melodies move predominantly stepwise which tends to make Palestrina's melodies easily singable. Notice the basically stepwise movement of the opening Kyrie in the soprano part.

D. **Harmony**
The actual number of harmonies used by Palestrina in this Mass movement is small. Basically, only major and minor triads in root position and their first inversions are employed.

E. **Cadences**
Palestrina ends each invocation with a different cadence; all three represent Palestrina and Renaissance vocal music generally.

> *Examples*
> Kyrie eleison   V-I
> Christe eleison   ii-I
> Kyrie eleison   IV-I

F. **Mode**
Ionian on F.

G. **Texture**
The imitative treatment of each invocation, that is, "Kyrie eleison," "Christe eleison," and "Kyrie eleison," shows the influence of the Netherlands school on Palestrina's music.

VII. Additional Source
Palestrina, Giovanni Pierluigi da. *Werke*. Edited by Franz X. Haberl et al. 33 vols. Leipzig: Breitkopf und Härtel, 1862-1900.

VIII. Recording
Palestrina. *Missa Assumpta est Maria, Missa Brevis for Four Voices*. Argo Record Co. 2RG.690.

Missa brevis.

Edited by
FRANK DAMROSCH.

G. P. da PALESTRINA.

15052 ×

Example 20. "Kyrie" from *Missa Brevis* by G. P. Palestrina. International copyright secured. All rights reserved. Reprinted by permission.

2

Christe eleison.
Soli or Semichorus.
Più lento. (♩ = 76.)

Kyrie Eleison.
Full Chorus.

"Agnus Dei" from *Missa Veni sponsa Christi*

I. **Title of Composition**
"Agnus Dei" from the *Missa Veni sponsa Christi*

II. **Type of Composition**
Mass movement

III. **Composer**
Giovanni Pierluigi da Palestrina (circa 1526-94) was an Italian composer of the late Renaissance who maintained a purity of style and a mastery of contrapuntal structure throughout his composing career. He began his musical study as a choirboy at Santa Maria Maggiore in Rome. In 1544 he became musical director at the cathedral in Palestrina, whose bishop became Pope Julius III. The pope brought Palestrina to Rome where the new decrees on simplifying sacred music found fruition in the composer's forthright style. Palestrina composed over 100 Masses, some 450 motets, 42 psalm settings, various Magnificats, litanies, and Lamentations, as well as some 200 sacred and secular madrigals.

IV. **Text and Translation**
Both the Latin text and English translation appear under Texts in the introductory information for the Renaissance Mass.

V. **Background**
From 1400 to 1600 many musical Masses were based on motets. This type of Mass, such as Palestrina's *Missa Veni sponsa Christi* ("Come, Bride of Christ"), is known as a Parody Mass. Palestrina had earlier written a motet based on a Gregorian refrain, and for his Mass he borrowed freely from the motet, sometimes using entire sections in their original form and sometimes varying the melodies. In the section under Melody, Palestrina's use of the Gregorian melody in the "Agnus Dei" of this Mass will be examined.

VI. **Structural and Stylistic Elements**

    A. **Medium**
        Agnus Dei I: Soprano, alto, tenor, and bass.
        Agnus Dei II: Soprano, alto, tenor I and II, and bass.

    B. **Meter**
        Duple.

C.   Rhythm

There is a gently marked regularity of rhythm which is characteristic of Palestrina's style. The collective rhythm heard when all the voices are sounding together gives the impression of a fairly regular succession of duple "measures" caused mainly be changes of harmony and placing suspensions on "strong" beats.

D.   Melody

Many of Palestrina's Masses are built on themes from Gregorian chant. The motet which served as the basis for this Mass was based on a Gregorian antiphon melody which is as follows:

Example 21. Antiphon: "Veni sponsa Christi."

The chant appears in the "Agnus Dei I" in the following places:

m.m. 1-9	"Agnus Dei" in each voice uses the theme of "Veni sponsa Christi." It appears transposed in the alto and bass, however.
m.m. 13-19	"Qui tollis" in alto and tenor is based on the Gregorian melody at "accipe coronam."
m.m. 19-25	"Miserere" in all voices is based on the Gregorian "quam tibi Dominus."

E.   Harmony

Palestrina's harmony basically consists of triads and chords of the sixth, or first inversion triads. Donald Grout points out in his book *A History of Western Music* that the combinations F-A-C or A-C-F occur twenty-one times in the "Agnus Dei I" alone. The use of triadic harmonies and little use of dissonance gives Palestrina's music a serene and transparent quality.

F.   Texture
The imitative contrapuntal style and the use of canon in this movement show the influence of the Netherlands school in Palestrina's music.

VII. Additional Source

Palestrina, Giovanni Pierluigi da. *Werke*. Edited by Franz X. Haberl et al. 33 vols. Leipzig: Breitkopf und Härtel, 1862-1900.

Agnus Dei I

Example 22. Courtesy of Edwin F. Kalmus and Co., Inc., Boca Raton, Fla.

Agnus Dei II

The Anthem

General Information

The English anthem is in many respects the Protestant Church's equivalent of the Latin motet. When the Church of England separated from the Roman Catholic communion in 1534 under Henry VIII, changes in language and liturgy took place. After Elizabeth I ascended to the throne in 1558, she requested the singing of "a hymn or suchlike song in churches," and the anthem of the English Tudor composers—named for Owen Tudor who married the widow of Henry V—came into prominence. Anthems differed from Latin motets mainly in their use of English. These unaccompanied, choral compositions were written from the time of the Reformation until the end of the great English choral school about 1660. Well-known composers of the "full" anthem were Thomas Tallis, William Byrd, Thomas Weelkes, and the father of Anglican church music, Orlando Gibbons. Another type of anthem called the "verse" anthem, in which soloists and instrumental accompaniment were employed, was introduced by William Byrd and brought to perfection by Orlando Gibbons in the late sixteenth and early seventeenth centuries. This type of anthem became the most popular form of music for the church service during the seventeenth century.

Texts

The texts for anthems were selected from the Scriptures, from the Book of Common Prayer, and from various sources such as poems of a religious nature. Many Tudor composers wrote music to Latin texts with English translations.

Performance

Although very little has been written about the performance of English anthems as such, it is assumed that they were performed very much as motets were. We know that they, like Latin motets, were often performed with organ and/or viols doubling the voice parts. As with all music of the Renaissance, dynamics should be employed with restraint. All tempo and dynamic markings which appear in the anthem for study and performance are suggestions made by the editor. It should be kept in mind that women's voices were not used to perform sacred music in the Renaissance. The soprano and alto parts were sung by boys, countertenors, and men singing falsetto. Therefore, when women do sing motets, Masses, and anthems today, they should always strive for as clear and light a voice quality as possible.

"Why Art Thou So Heavy, O My Soul?"

I. Title of Composition
"Why Art Thou So Heavy, O My Soul?"

II. Type of Composition
English full anthem

III. Composer
Orlando Gibbons* (1583-1625) was without equal in the area of English church music. He was born in Oxford, England, and began his musical career in 1596 as a choirboy at King's College, Cambridge. He became organist of the Chapel Royal in 1605, and in 1606 he was graduated from Cambridge. Toward the end of his life, in 1623, he became organist of Westminster Abbey. Two years later he died suddenly at Canterbury where, with the rest of the Chapel Royal, he had gone to prepare the music for the wedding of Charles I. Gibbons not only excelled as a composer of anthems but was also an excellent composer of madrigals, string, and keyboard music. His forty anthems for the Anglican church are published in Volume 4 of *Tudor Church Music*.

IV. Text
The text for this anthem is Psalm 43:5,6. It should be read by conductor and performers for clues concerning proper tempo and dynamics. The indications which appear in the music are all editorial (there being none in the original) and merely serve as suggestions for performance.

V. Background
Of the forty anthems composed by Gibbons, only fifteen were full; the rest are verse anthems. "Why Art Thou So Heavy, O My Soul?" is typical of the contrapuntal full anthem brought to fruition by Gibbons at the end of the sixteenth and beginning of the seventeenth century.

---

*Please note this new edition (on pp. 165-168), edited by Cyril F. Simkins, attributes this anthem to Henry Loosemore (see "Editor's note" on p. 165 for details).

VI. **Structural and Stylistic Elements**

    A. **Medium**
    Soprano, alto, tenor, and bass.

    B. **Meter**
    Duple. Metrical accent is foreign to this style. Although the music does proceed in duple meter, there should be no feeling of a strong one- and weak two-beat.

    C. **Rhythm**
    Polyrhythmic sections, sections in which the individual voices move in different rhythms, are the norm for this anthem except for one short section in homorhythm, a section in which the voices move in the same rhythm except for slight variations in one or two voices.

    Example
    mm. 14-21.

    D. **Texture**
    Except for the basically homophonic-homorhythmic section mentioned above, this anthem's texture is imitative counterpoint, that is, it uses the same thematic material in all the voice parts. The opening section is a perfect example of real imitation so evident in contrapuntal music before 1550 in which each voice enters in an exact transposition of the first voice, or theme. This real imitation accounts for the use of C natural in both the alto and bass parts in the opening section.

    E. **Cadences**
    A change of tonal focus was usually achieved in Renaissance music by cadencing on various degrees of the mode. Notice the following cadences at the end of specific phrases:

    Examples
    mm. 11-12   V-I in B Major.
    m. 18   V-I in D Major.
    mm. 20-21   V-I in A Major.
    mm. 33-34   IV-I in B Major.

    F. **Entrances**
    The voices enter in descending order—soprano, alto, tenor, and bass; they enter alternately on the dominant and final B of the transposed mode.

G.   **Imitation**

An important element in imitation is the amount of time which elapses between the successive entries of the voices. In the sacred music of the Renaissance it is rare to find successive voices entering regularly one or two measures apart. Gibbons first presents the theme on the first beat of the measure in the soprano, and this is answered in the middle of the first measure by the alto. In the sixth measure the tenor sings the theme, and this is answered in the middle of the same measure by the bass. Such entrances are said to be staggered, that is, the voices are spaced irregularly which actually allows the beginning of phrases (words) to be more clearly understood.

H.   **Form**

Each line of the text is set to a melodic theme which permeates and tends to unify the section by its frequent appearance in all or most of the voices. In this anthem Gibbons sets the text phrase by phrase with each phrase having its own theme which is developed. The text is divided into three sections and an *Amen*: 1) "Why art thou so heavy, o my soul, and why art thou so disquieted within me?"; 2) "O put thy trust in God"; 3) "for I will give him thanks, which is the help of my countenance and my God"; 4) *Amen*.

VII. Text Setting

Basically syllabic, one syllable to each note or chord. The final *Amen* section is melismatic, many notes to one syllable.

VIII. Additional Source

Tudor Church Music. Edited by P. C. Buck, E. H. Fellowes, A. Ramsbotham, R. R. Terry, and S. Townsend Warner. 10 vols. London: Oxford University Press, 1922-1929. Vol. 4. *Orlando Gibbons.*

Why Art Thou So Heavy, O My Soul?

SATB

HENRY LOOSEMORE, d. 1670
Formerly ascribed to ORLANDO GIBBONS, c. 1583–1625
Transcribed and edited by CYRIL F. SIMKINS

Psalm 43: 5,6

This piece has been transposed up a whole tone from the original, and note values halved.
All tempo and expression marks are editorial.

Editor's note: When this work was first discovered the music-text source was that given in Tudway's *Collection of Cathedral Music, Vol. 4* (Harley Manuscript 7337, 1715–20), where the composer was listed as Orlando Gibbons. In more recent times, an earlier source (Drexel Manuscript 5469, New York Public Library, c. 1630) has been brought to light and the composition listed as the work of Henry Loosemore. Loosemore was appointed organist at King's College, Cambridge, in 1627 until his death in 1670, when Thomas Tudway succeeded him.

Transcribed from British Museum Add Manuscripts (Harley 7337—fo. 136).

Copyright © 1979 Concordia Publishing House, St. Louis, Mo.
98-2437   All Rights Reserved   Printed in U.S.A.

Example 23. Reprinted by permission of Concordia Publishing House, St. Louis, Missouri. Copyright 1979.

* The original shows this and the final measure in $\frac{6}{4}$.

4

and my ___ God, which is the help ___ of my coun-te-nance and my ___

___ and ___ my God, which ___ is the help of ___ my coun-te-nance and ___

___ my God, which is the help of ___ my coun-te-nance and

___ my God, which is the help of my coun-te-nance and ___

___ God. A - men, a - men, a - men.

___ my God. A - men, a - men.

my God. A - men.

___ my God. A men, ___ a - men.

The Chorale Motet

General Information

In German Protestant music of the Reformation, a chorale was a musical setting of a hymn or psalm which was meant to be sung by the congregation. It was introduced into the service by Martin Luther (1483-1546), who wrote texts and melodies for chorales. It was Luther's strong conviction that the congregation should take some part in the music of the service, and the chorale enabled them to do so. From the Reformation until the present, musical compositions have been based on popular religious chorale melodies. Protestant German composers at the end of the sixteenth century began to use chorale melodies as the basic material for free artistic creation. At this time the chorale motet came into being. These melodies were not always used throughout a composition in unchanged form, however. Composers of the chorale motet began to break away from the traditional tunes, although they did use melodic material which was related to the chorale. Donald Grout, author of *A History of Western Music*, points out that the appearance of the chorale motet confirmed the division which has existed ever since in Protestant church music between simple congregational hymns and more elaborate music for a trained choir. The main German composers of chorale motets were Hans Leo Hassler, Johannes Eccard, Leonhard Lechner, and Michael Praetorius.

Texts

Luther, as well as others, wrote chorale texts. Texts were also made up entirely or in part from existing sacred and secular songs. It was not uncommon to add new words to a popular song of the day and thereby give it religious meaning. One of the most famous examples of this type of "parody" chorale is Isaac's Lied "Innsbruck, I Now Must Leave Thee," to which the words "O World, I Now Must Leave Thee" were substituted. Another major source of chorale texts was the Roman liturgy translated into German.

Performance

The information given under Performance for the Renaissance motet would also serve as a guide for the performance of the chorale motet.

"Psallite"
("Sing Your Psalms")

I. Title of Composition
"Psallite" ("Sing Your Psalms")

II. Type of Composition
Chorale motet

III. Composer
Michael Praetorius (1571-1621) was in the service of the Duke of Brunswick at Groningen from 1589 and Wolfenbüttel from 1604. He was one of the most prolific composers of his time, composing large numbers of sacred songs, motets, madrigals, and litanies. Praetorius contributed to instrumental literature with his publication of dances, *Terpsichore* (1612), and with his great treatise *Syntagma Musicum* (1615-1620), the second volume of which dealt with instruments and their functions. The third and last volume dealt with methods of performance and choir-training and offers valuable insights into the performance practices of Renaissance music in general.

IV. Text
The text is a combination of Latin and German phrases. An English translation also appears in the music.

V. Background
In 1605 Praetorius began the publication of *Musae Sioniae*, or "Muses from Sion," a collection in nine volumes of 1,244 of his compositions based on chorales. The chorale settings range from *bicinia* (two-part songs) to settings for quadruple choirs. In the preface to the ninth volume, Praetorius described three main methods of treating the chorale melodies: 1) the "chorale motet," each phrase of the melody being used as a point of imitation in the older polyphonic style; 2) the "madrigal-fashion," in which the chorale is split into small motifs that are employed in dialogue between groups of voices; and 3) the *cantus firmus* setting, in which the chorale in long notes forms a *cantus firmus* around which other voices are woven. Although "Psallite" is not specifically attributed to Praetorius, it appears in the sixth volume of *Musae Sioniae*. The treatment given to the chorale melody seems to fall between the motet and madrigal styles of chorale treatment described by Praetorius.

VI. Structural and Stylistic Elements

   A. Medium
   Soprano, alto, tenor, and bass.

170

    B.   **Melody**
       Each voice enters with a descending perfect fourth which is heard in each voice on the word *Psallite*. Otherwise, the voices move basically by step or in conjunct motion.

    C.   **Texture**
       Imitation and homophony are evident throughout. The texture is often varied by voice pairings, that is, soprano and alto sing a phrase which is answered by tenor and bass.

    D.   **Mode**
       Ionian mode on G.

    E.   **Form**
       ABA'

VII. Additional Source
    Praetorius, Michael. *Gesamtausgabe der musikalischen Werke.* Edited by F. Blume, W. Gurlitt, and A. Mendelssohn. 20 vols. Wolfenbüttel: Gikallpaeyer Verlag, 1928-40.

VIII. Recording
    From Heaven Above, The Deller Consort, Alfred Deller, Director, No. RCA Vics-1376.

Psallite

Sing Your Psalms

Tr., P. T.

Composer unknown
Musae Sioniae, VI, 1609

98-1869

Example 24. Reprinted by permission of Concordia Publishing House, St. Louis, Missouri. Copyright 1962.

4

Chri - sto, De - i Fi - li - o. Psal - li - te
Je - sus Christ, the Son of God. Sing your psalms

Chri - sto, De - i Fi - li - o,
Je - sus Christ, the Son of God,

Chri - sto, De - i Fi - li - o,
Je - sus Christ, the Son of God,

Chri - sto, De - i Fi - li - o,
Je - sus Christ, the Son of God,

Re - demp - to - ri, Do - mi - no, pu - e - ru - lo ia - cen - ti
to the blest Re - deem - er, Lord, the ho - ly Child now ly - ing

Re - demp - to - ri, Do - mi - no, pu - e - ru - lo ia - cen - ti
to the blest Re - deem - er, Lord, the ho - ly Child now ly - ing

Re - demp - to - ri, Do - mi - no, pu - e - ru - lo ia - cen - ti
to the blest Re - deem - er, Lord, the ho - ly Child now ly - ing

Re - demp - to - ri, Do - mi - no, pu - e - ru - lo ia - cen - ti
to the blest Re - deem - er, Lord, the ho - ly Child now ly - ing

in prae - se - pi - o.   Ein klei - nes Kin - de - lein liegt in dem Krip - pe-
in a man - ger - bed.   Come, see the In-fant small A - cra - dled in the

in prae - se - pi - o.   Ein klei - nes Kin - de - lein liegt in dem Krip - pe-
in a man - ger - bed.   Come, see the In-fant small A - cra - dled in the

in prae - se - pi - o. _____
in a man - ger - bed. _____

in prae - se - pi - o. _____
in a man - ger - bed. _____

lein;   Al - le
stall;   An - gel

lein;   Al - le
stall;   An - gel

Al - le lie - ben En - ge - lein die - nen dem Kin - de - lein und sin-
An - gel hosts in heav'n-ly hall Be - fore His foot-stool fall, Sing - ing

Al - le lie - ben En - ge - lein die - nen dem Kin - de - lein und sin-
An - gel hosts in heav'n-ly hall Be - fore His foot-stool fall, Sing - ing

6

98-1869

The Performer's Workbook

Introduction

The Renaissance—that period in music from approximately 1425 to 1625—was one of the most exciting periods in history. The music you will sing and study represents some of the best examples of Renaissance literature. The purpose of this workbook is to help you look more closely at the music* in order to come to a better understanding of it. Four questions have been posed for each piece. The answers appear immediately following the questions so you will know if your responses were correct. A musical activity also appears after the questions, which will allow you to think more critically about the music you are preparing for performance.

The music in this unit was prepared by modern editors. Composers in the Renaissance used no bar lines, dynamic or tempo markings. Bar lines have been added to help you sing the music more easily; dynamic and tempo markings are merely suggestions for performance. Vocal music in the Renaissance was usually composed for specific occasions and for either a small choir or a group of soloists. Because of this, the music should be performed in a restrained manner. With these things in mind, sing, learn, and enjoy it!

---

*The use G, g, g′, and g″ in referring to different octaves is used throughout this workbook. G refers to the bottom line of the bass clef; g to the octave above; g′ to the second line of the treble clef; and g″ to the octave above that.

Josquin Desprez's "Mille regretz" ("Deep Is My Grief")

1. Josquin (zhoss-can), the only composer to be called affectionately by his first name, wrote some seventy songs or chansons with French texts. Chansons were a popular type of vocal music composed throughout the Renaissance. According to the Introduction to "The Performer's Workbook," how was the vocal music of this time performed? Write your answer in the space below.

2. Renaissance composers did not put tempo markings in their music, although the human heart beat, that is, 60-80 beats per minute, served as a guide. Within that limit, it was the mood of the text that largely determined the speed of a composition. After carefully reading the text of Josquin's chanson, which of the following do you consider the most appropriate tempo? Circle your answer.

   very slow   moderately slow   moderately fast

3. Josquin often varied the texture of his music by having the voices sing in pairs. Soprano and alto would sing a phrase which was answered by tenor and bass, or vice versa. Look at the music and state in which measures this technique occurs.

4. Renaissance composers used nonharmonic tones, that is, tones not belonging to the basic harmony, in their music. Two of the most frequently used nonharmonic tones in Renaissance music are 1) passing tones and 2) neighbor tones. Study the examples of both given below. Then find 1) the passing tones in the soprano and bass in measure 3 of "Mille regretz" and 2) the neighbor tones in the soprano and bass in measure 4.

   1) Passing tone
      Usually moves on weak part of beat.
      Always moves by step from one consonance to another.
      Always continues in the direction by which it is approached.

   Example 1. Passing tone.

2)   Neighbor tone
Usually moves on weak part of beat.
Always moves by step from one harmony note to another.
Always turns back to the note it just left.

Example 2. Neighbor tone, upper and lower.

Answers

1.   Vocal music in the Renaissance was performed by either a small choir or a group of soloists. The secular (nonreligious) music was usually performed by soloists.

2.   The emotions expressed in the text of Josquin's chanson are basically those of pain and grief. A moderately slow tempo seems the most appropriate for this composition.

3.   Measures 19-24:   Soprano and alto are answered by tenor and bass.

4.   Passing tone: Measure 3   e' in soprano and c in bass.
     Neighbor tone: Measure 4   c' in soprano and a in bass.

Activity
Look carefully at the editorial markings in Josquin's chanson. Make a list of all that are used (dynamics, crescendos, etc.). Form a small group of four singers each, soprano, alto, tenor, and bass, and discuss whether or not you think the editorial markings are appropriate as they relate to the text. Since none were present in the original, your conclusions will all be "correct." If time permits, add your own dynamic markings and sing this chanson using your own ideas. Are they different from the editor's? Approximately the same? Discuss your conclusions.

Claudin de Sermisy's
"J'ay fait pour vous cent mille pas"
("A Hundred Thousand Steps")

1. Chanson is the French word for song. In French-speaking countries the word chanson has always been used to describe any song composed on a French text. Therefore, Sermisy's song, "J'ay fair pour vous cent mille pas" ("A Hundred Thousand Steps") is a French
    _____.

2. Sermisy's chanson was written for soprano, alto, tenor, and bass. Slightly different names for these voice parts were used in the Renaissance, and they appear at the beginning of your music. The soprano part was called the _____; the alto was known as the _____; the tenor was called the _____, just as it is today; and the bass was known as the _____.

3. In Sermisy's chansons, the character of the text largely determined the character of the music. After reading the text for this song, circle the two words which best describe the character of the music.

    expressive   dramatic   instrumental   singable

4. The text for this chanson is a stanza of five lines. Each line of text is set to one phrase of music; therefore, there are five musical phrases. You can determine the musical form of this chanson by following the text and the music. Using letters, the musical form is A , _____, _____,
    _____, _____.

Answers

1. Sermisy's "J'ay fait pour vous cent mille pas" is a French chanson.

2. The soprano part was called the *superius* (soo-perr'-i-oos); the alto was known as the *contratenor*, or *contratenor altus*; the tenor was known as it is today; and the bass was called the *bassus*, or *contratenor bassus*.

3. The musical character of this chanson is expressive and singable rather than dramatic and instrumental. The Italian term used to describe the "singable" quality of music is *cantabile* (cahn-tah'-bee-leh).

4. Following the five lines of the text and noting the musical phrases, the musical form is A - A - B - C - C.

Activity

Now that you know the form of Sermisy's chanson, place the correct letters at the beginning of each section in your music. Renaissance verse set to music is filled with as much passion as is the music of the Romantic period some two hundred years later. Based on your own feelings about life and love, try writing a poem using the form of Sermisy's chanson. You may share it with the class or not—the choice is yours.

Guillaume Costeley's
"Allon, gay Bergeres"
("Come, Gay Shepherds")

1. A popular Christmas song with French text, such as Costeley's "Allon, Gay Bergeres," is known as a _____.

2. This song by Costeley (cot-lay) is probably one of the earliest examples of rondo form, characterized by the alternation of a recurrent refrain with various verses. "Allon, gay Bergeres" is the refrain, and this section is referred to as "A." How many times does the refrain appear? The first verse is referred to as "B," the second as "C," and so on. Using letters, what is the form of this chanson?

   The refrain or "A" section appears _____ times.
   The form of the entire chanson is _____.

3. When all the voices in a composition move in the same rhythm, the composition is said to be *homorhythmic*, which literally means "same rhythm." When all the voices move in different rhythms, the composition is said to be *polyrhythmic*, which literally means "many rhythms." Which sections of this chanson are homorhythmic and which sections are polyrhythmic? Write your answers below:

4. Costeley begins this chanson in D minor and ends it in D major. A D-major scale looks like this:

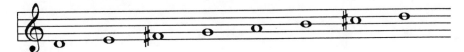

Example 3. D major scale.

Look at the last two notes in the bass at the end of the piece. Which notes of the scale are they on? Write your answer below.

Example 4. Costeley, "Allon, Gay Bergeres," p. 10, mm. 52-55.

Answers

1.   A Christmas song with French text is known as a noël.

2.   The refrain or "A" section appears five times. Using letters, the form of this song is A - B - A - C - A - D - A - E - A.

3.   The refrains are *homorhythmic* and the verses are *polyrhythmic*.

4.   The bass ends on the 4th and 1st degrees of the scale. This produces a IV-I cadence, which is a very important one in Renaissance music.

Activity

Chansons were frequently performed on instruments alone or with one solo voice and instruments. Performances in which instruments and voices are combined are not only interesting but enjoyable as well. Select four instrumentalists to cover the voice parts—soprano, alto, tenor, and bass. How many different ways can chansons be performed using voices and/or instruments? Jot down your ideas and enjoy the performances. Help dispel the myth that all Renaissance music was performed "a cappella."

Jacob Arcadelt's
"Voi ve n'andat' al cielo"
("Now to the Heavens Are Turning")

1. This composition by Arcadelt is an Italian _____. It is scored for four voices which, reading from top to bottom, are _____, _____, _____, and _____.

2. Because no sections of Arcadelt's madrigal are repeated, the form is _____.

3. Renaissance composers, especially the Italian madrigalists, were very much aware of the texts they were setting to music. They used three basic styles of text settings: *syllabic*, one note or chord to one syllable of text; *neumatic*, several notes to one syllable of text; and *melismatic*, numerous notes to one syllable of text. Which style of text setting did Arcadelt use for this madrigal? Circle your answer.

    melismatic   neumatic   syllabic

4. The word *cadence* literally means "falling." The name probably comes from the fact that it has almost always been customary for a melody to end by falling to the tonic, or first degree of the scale. For a cadence to be called *perfect*, the last chord must be the tonic triad (I) and must have the tonic note in the soprano. When the preceding or penultimate chord is built on the fifth scale-degree (V), the combination of V-I is called an *authentic* cadence.

    A perfect authentic cadence in Arcadelt's madrigal will look like this:

    Example 5. Arcadelt, "Voi ve n'andat' al cielo," p. 10, mm. 61-64.

    How many perfect authentic cadences can you locate in this madrigal? Play the above example on the piano several times and begin to listen for it in all the music you hear.

Answers

1. This composition is an Italian madrigal. It is scored for soprano, alto, tenor, and bass.

2. The form is through-composed.

3. The style of text setting is syllabic, one syllable of text to one note or chord of music.

4. There are three perfect authentic cadences in this composition.

    a. Last beat of m. 11 and first beat of m. 12.
    b. Last two beats of m. 57 and the first two beats of m. 58.
    c. Last two beats of m. 63 and all of m. 64.

Activity

The two major textures used by Arcadelt in this madrigal are *homophonic* and *polyphonic*. Look up these two terms in a music dictionary, such as *The New Harvard Dictionary of Music*, edited by Don Michael Randel in 1986. The publisher is the Belknap Press of Harvard University Press, Cambridge, Massachusetts. This most important resource should be in your school library. If not, ask for it! It is also available or can be ordered through your local bookstore.

Write down your definitions of *homophonic* and *polyphonic*. Now look carefully at the opening measures of this madrigal. Is it polyphonic or homophonic? Why?

Now look at mm. 25-35. Which texture is used? Why?

Using these two terms, how would you describe the texture used in other places in this work? Also, what is the texture of a hymn or folk song? What is the texture of a fugue? Aren't sure? Remember *The New Harvard!*

Cipriano de Rore's
"Da le belle contrade d'Oriente"
("From the Fair Realms of the East")

1. Read the English translation provided for you. Each four lines is called a stanza or strophe. When each stanza is sung to the same music, as in a hymn or folk song, the form is said to be *strophic*. When different music is used for each stanza, the form is *through-composed*. There are four sections to this madrigal: mm. 1-16; 17-31; 32-41; and 42-62. Each stanza is set to the *same/different* music (circle the correct answer). Therefore, the form is _____.

2. Rore's most famous madrigals were composed for five voices. Look at the first four measures. The first voice to enter is the _____; the second voice to enter is the _____; the third and fourth voices to enter together are the _____ and _____; and the last voice to enter in m. 4 is _____. Therefore, the opening texture is imitative or polyphonic, not homophonic or chordal.

3. As you sing this madrigal by Rore, you will notice that each voice part has a number of accidentals, that is, signs which are used to alter certain notes. Rore's use of accidentals allowed him to express more fully the text in his music, a technique known as "word painting."

    The three accidentals used in this madrigal are 1) ♯, 2) ♭, and 3) ♮. Using those symbols, answer the following:

    A ___ raises a tone one half-step.
    A ___ lowers a tone one half-step.
    A ___ cancels either of the above.

4. After 1550, it was customary in Renaissance vocal music to end all compositions with a major triad (or without a third in the chord at all) rather than with a minor triad. Look at the final chord of Rore's madrigal. Is it a complete major triad (G-B-D) or is the B, or third, missing?

Answers

1.   Each stanza is set to *different* music. Therefore, the form is through-composed.

2.   The voices enter Tenor 1, Alto, Soprano and Bass, and Tenor 2 in m. 4.

3.   A ♯ raises a tone one half-step.

      A ♭ lowers a tone one half-step.

      A ♮ cancels out either a sharp or flat.

4.   The final chord is a major triad: G-B-D. Bass-G; Tenor 2-D; Tenor 1-G; Alto-B; and Soprano-G.

Activity
The class will be divided into groups of three singers each. Each singer will have a copy of Rore's madrigal "Da le belle contrade d'Oriente." The purpose of this activity is to come to a better understanding of the Renaissance technique known as *musica reservata*, or "word painting." Composers in the Renaissance used chromaticism, or accidentals, to help paint or "color" the text they were setting to music. Make a list of these words which Rore changed by chromaticism. How has chromaticism allowed Rore to "color" the text? Look carefully at the English translation to help you discover the words that are altered. How does this change the meaning of the text and why? Share your conclusions with the other groups. It will also be helpful to look up the terms *musica reservata* and *chromaticism* in a music dictionary.

Luca Marenzio's
"Già torna a rallegrar"
("Now Once More to All the Earth")

1. Renaissance composers, especially the Italian madrigalists, were very much aware of the texts they were setting to music. One of the main characteristics of Marenzio's madrigals is the specific way in which the music expresses the words or ideas suggested by the text. This technique is known as _____.

2. Marenzio scored this madrigal for five voices. The voices enter in descending order from top to bottom. The entrances are _____, _____, _____, _____, and _____.

3. Since no sections of this madrigal are repeated, the form is _____.

4. Word painting is evident throughout this composition. Jot down the ways you think Marenzio has treated the following words in the music:

    a. mm. 25-29. *Il mar* is the Italian for "the sea." How does the movement of the melodic lines express this?

    b. mm. 29-31. *S'acqueta* is the Italian for "quieting" or "calm." What texture does Marenzio use to express that word?

    c. mm. 32-39. *Sotterra* is the Italian word for "underground." How does the movement of the vocal lines express this thought?

    d. What other examples of word painting can you find in Marenzio's madrigal?

Answers

1.   When the music expresses the text, the technique is known as word painting.

2.   Soprano I, soprano II, alto, tenor, and bass.

3.   The form of this madrigal is through-composed.

4.   a.   *Il mar* is represented by wavy melodic lines in all the voices.

        b.   *S'acqueta* is given a chordal texture which gives the music a feeling of "quiet" after the previous motion on the word for "sea."

        c.   *Sotterra* is treated with descending scale passages to express the feeling of frost melting into the earth.

        d.   Other examples of word painting are:

                i)   mm. 56-71: *piango*, or "weep," is expressed by long note values and descending melodic lines.

                ii)   mm. 72-79: faster note values are used to express the final phrase of text—"Soon will the sun unveil the welcome morrow."

Activity
From your study of Marenzio's madrigal, it is understandable that his use of word painting was considered outstanding in his day as well as in ours. Compare Marenzio's use of chromaticism with that of Rore. Is there more chromaticism in Rore's madrigal than in Marenzio's? Is chromaticism necessary for a composer to "paint" a text? Compare and contrast your findings with those of other members of the class.

Giovanni Gastoldi's
"Il bell' humore"
("Good Humor")

1.   Now that you have sung Gastoldi's "Il bell' humore," write a definition of *balletto* based upon your work with this form.

2.   When all the voices in a composition move in the same rhythm, the composition is said to be homorhythmic, which literally means "same rhythm." When this occurs, the text setting is usually syllabic, which means that one syllable of text is set to one chord or note. Is Gastoldi's *balletto* homorhythmic throughout? Is the text setting syllabic throughout? If any differences occur, where are they?

3.   The texture of most Renaissance music is either homophonic or polyphonic. In a homophonic texture one voice leads melodically with the other voices serving as a kind of accompaniment. In a polyphonic texture all the voices are equally important. What is the basic texture of Gastoldi's *balletto*? Circle your answer.

           polyphonic   homophonic

4.   When all stanzas of the text are sung to the same music, the form is said to be strophic. When there is different music for each stanza, the form is said to be through-composed. Since both stanzas of this balletto are sung to the same music, the form is _____.

Answers

1.   A *balletto* is a composition for voices and/or instruments. It is mainly homophonic and has a "fa-la" refrain.

2.   This composition is homorhythmic except for the "fa-la" refrain which is slightly different. The text setting is syllabic throughout.

3.   The texture is homophonic or chordal throughout, except for the "fa-la" refrain which is slightly more polyphonic.

4.   The form is strophic since the same music is used for each stanza.

Activity
All Italian *balletti* may be performed by voices and instruments in a variety of ways:

1.   All parts may be sung *a cappella.*
2.   All parts may be sung and doubled on instruments such as recorders, strings, or other combinations of instruments.
3.   One of the soprano parts may be performed as a solo accompanied by a keyboard instrument or guitar.

Perform this *balletto* in the various styles. Do you prefer one over the others? Why? Share your feelings with the other members of the class.

William Byrd's
"I Thought that Love Had Been a Boy"

1. The form of the madrigal that developed in Italy during the sixteenth century did not become popular in England until 1588, when a collection of Italian madrigals with English texts was published there. The form then flourished in the hands of such well-known English composers as Byrd, Morley, and Weelkes. This composition by Byrd which you have sung is an excellent example of the English _____, and is scored for _____, _____, _____, _____, and _____.

2. The melodies found in Renaissance music are considered to be very singable. This is due primarily to the fact that they tend to move by step, although skips are added for variety. When a melody moves mainly by step, it is said to be *conjunct*; when it moves by skip, it is said to be *disjunct*. Look at the part you have sung in this madrigal. Is it basically conjunct or disjunct? Circle your conclusion.

conjunct   disjunct

3. The texture of most Renaissance music is either homophonic or polyphonic. In a homophonic texture one voice leads melodically with the other voices serving as a kind of accompaniment. In a polyphonic texture all the voices are equally important. After having sung Byrd's madrigal, would you say that the texture is more homophonic or polyphonic? Circle your conclusion.

polyphonic   homophonic

4. A *perfect authentic* cadence occurs when there is a V-I progression is the bass voice and the tonic note is in the soprano. A *perfect authentic* cadence in Byrd's madrigal looks like the following:

Example 6. Perfect authentic cadence.

Is the cadence at the end of m. 18 and the beginning of m. 19 a perfect authentic cadence? Is the cadence at the end of the piece a perfect authentic cadence? Explain why they are or are not.

Answers

1. This composition is an English madrigal and is scored for soprano I, soprano II, alto, tenor, and bass.

2. All the voices are basically conjunct, with the possible exception of the bass.

3. The texture is more homophonic and chordal than polyphonic.

4. The cadence at mm. 18 and 19 is a perfect authentic cadence because of the V-I movement in the bass and the tonic note (f′) in the soprano. The final cadence is not perfect because the third of the triad, rather than the tonic note, is in the soprano.

Activity
The poems written during the sixteenth century were of exceptional quality. The poems of Edmund Spenser (circa 1552-99) and his followers, Sir Walter Raleigh (circa 1552-1618) and Sir Philip Sidney (1554-86) set a new standard for English madrigal verse. Can you name other English poets and playwrights during that period? Go to your school library, make a list of them, and then select a poem or sonnet you feel would be suitable to set to music. Are you a composer? Why not try to set the poem you have selected to your own music? Only a minimum amount of music theory is needed to do this successfully. You can start by composing a simple melody (c′-c″; d′-d″, etc.), and perhaps later add a simple accompaniment. If possible, perform your composition for the class.

Thomas Morley's "Sing We and Chant It"

1. The *balletto* originated in Italy at the end of the sixteenth century. In 1591, the Italian composer Gastoldi published a collection of *balletti* which he maintained could be sung, played on instruments, and danced. The form was imitated in other countries, but most skillfully by Thomas Morley in England. Now that you have sung this delightful piece of music, write a definition of this form, which was known in England as a ballett.

2. The texture of most Renaissance music is either homophonic or polyphonic. In a homophonic texture one voice leads melodically with the other voices serving as a kind of accompaniment. In a polyphonic texture all the voices are equally important. Morley uses two different textures in his ballett. As you look at the music, the verse is cast in a _____ texture, and the "fa-la" refrain appears to be more _____.

3. "Sing We and Chant It" has a text composed of two stanzas which are sung to the same music. Therefore, the form is _____.

4. Renaissance composers used nonharmonic tones, that is, tones not belonging to the basic harmony, in their music. One of the most characteristic nonharmonic tones found in Renaissance music is the *suspension*. The suspension is a dissonance found on an accented part of a measure. Suspensions involve three specific steps:

    1. **Preparation:**   *Always* on a weak beat.
    2. **Suspension:**   *Always* on the following strong beat.
    3. **Resolution:**   *Always* on the following weak beat.

    P-S-R refers to the movement of a single voice part.

Example 7. Suspension.

Now look at mm. 6 and 7. In which voice does the suspension occur?

Answers

1.   The ballett, like the *balletto*, is a composition for voices and/or instruments. It is mainly homophonic, with a polyphonic refrain.

2.   The verse is more homophonic-chordal, and the "fa-la" refrain is more polyphonic.

3.   Since the same music is used for both stanzas, the form is strophic.

4.   The suspension occurs in the second soprano.

Activity

All musics are an expression of the composer's thoughts and feelings. Composers use musical notation to express their thoughts just as poets use words. Now that you have sung Morley's ballett, take another careful look at the text. What is the mood of this piece? What do you think the poet is trying to express? Discuss your answers with the other members of the class.

Heinrich Isaac's "Innsbruck, ich muss dich lassen" ("Innsbruck, I Now Must Leave Thee")

1. Lied (leet) is the German word for "song" (Lieder [leed-er], "songs"). This Lied by Isaac is considered one of the most beautiful of the Renaissance. The melody was so appealing that sacred words were added so that it could be sung in German churches. The melody was used some two hundred years later by J. S. Bach for one of the chorales in his *St. Matthew Passion*. Both the text used by Isaac and the added sacred text appear in your music. The technique of adding new words to an existing melody is known as *contrafactum*. Write a brief definition of Lied.

2. Write a brief definition of *contrafactum*.

3. Renaissance composers used nonharmonic tones, that is, tones not belonging to the basic harmony, in their music. One of the most characteristic nonharmonic tones found in Renaissance music is the *suspension*. The suspension is a dissonance found on an accented part of a measure. Suspensions involve three specific steps:

    1. **Preparation:** *Always* on a weak beat.
    2. **Suspension:** *Always* on the following strong beat.
    3. **Resolution:** *Always* on the following weak beat.

    P-S-R refers to the movement of a single voice part.

    Example 8. Isaac, "Innsbruck, ich muss dich lassen," p. 3, mm. 1-3.

    A suspension occurs in the alto in mm. 2 and 3. Can you find other suspensions in this music? If so, where do they occur?

4. Since no sections are repeated in this composition, the form is _____.

Answers

1.   A Lied is a monophonic or polyphonic song with German text.

2.   When new words are added to existing songs, the technique is known as *contrafactum*.

3.   Suspensions occur in the alto in mm. 5 and 6; 9 and 10; 12 and 13; and in the soprano in mm. 15-16.

4.   The form is through-composed.

Activity
Lieder in the sixteenth century were often performed entirely on instruments. Instruments can be grouped in a "whole" or homogeneous consort or into a "broken" or heterogeneous consort, as they were called in the Renaissance. Are there enough instrumentalists in your group to try this? Play the SATB parts on all woodwinds, strings, or brass instruments. Then play this Lied using a variety of instruments, as was done in the "broken" consort. Does one performance appeal to you more than the other? Why or why not? Renaissance vocal music calls upon us to make musical choices, and these are often based solely on our musical tastes.

Ludwig Senfl's
"Wohlauf, jung und alt"
("Arise, Young and Old")

1.   This Lied by Senfl is based on not one, but several German folk tunes. This type of composition is known as a *quodlibet*, a Latin word which defines a humorous type of music in which well-known melodies are combined in no particular order. Many Renaissance compositions are based on one melody known as a *cantus firmus*, literally a "fixed song," around which composers created other melodies. However, this composition by Senfl is known as a

      _____.

2.   Notice the different textures Senfl uses to emphasize the text. The opening four measures are polyphonic/homophonic (circle the correct answer). Why? Whereas the texture of mm. 20-24 is clearly _____. Why?

3.   Name the interval used by Senfl in m. 3 of the soprano part on the word "Arise." This is an excellent example of word painting. Can you find other examples of an ascending interval on the word "Arise" in your own part? State specific measures.

4.   What well-known Renaissance technique is used in mm. 44-49?

Answers

1.   *Quodlibet.*

2.   Homophonic. The texture is chordal and the melody is in the soprano. Measures 20-24; the texture is polyphonic; both voices are equally important and imitative. The tenor is imitated by the bass.

3.   P4.
     Soprano—mm. 28; 29.
     Alto—not used.
     Tenor—mm. 1-4; 5-6; 27-29; 30-31.
     Bass—mm. 1-3; 4; 26-29.

4.   Word painting.

Activity
Now that you have sung the major secular forms of the Renaissance, write a short definition of each.

1.   The French chanson
2.   The Italian madrigal and *balletto*
3.   The English madrigal and ballett
4.   The German Lied

Hans Leo Hassler's
"Ach Schatz Ich Thu Dir Klagen"
("Oh Love, Hear Thou My Pleading")

1. Hans Leo Hassler is considered one of the greatest Renaissance composers of German Lieder (songs). His dates appear on the first page of your music; he was born in the year _____ and died in _____. He scored this Lied for five voices which, reading from top to bottom, are _____, _____, _____, _____, and _____.

2. Measures 1-14 comprise the first section of this Lied. Since these measures are repeated, the form for this first section is _____ ___. The second, or "B," section also begins in m. 14 and is repeated in the middle of m. 36 to the end of the piece. Therefore, the overall form for this Lied is A ___ ___ ___.

3. A *perfect authentic* cadence occurs when there is a V-I progression in the bass voice and the tonic note appears in the soprano. A perfect authentic cadence in this Lied will look like the following:

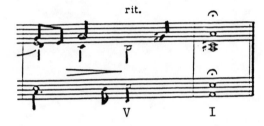

Example 9. mm. 57-58.

Is the cadence at the end of the "A" section (mm. 13-14) a perfect authentic cadence? Is the cadence at the end of the piece a perfect authentic cadence? Explain why they are or are not.

4. All tempo and dynamic markings in Renaissance music are placed there by modern editors and are merely suggestions for performance. The suggested tempo for this Lied is *andante,* and the dynamic level for the opening measures is *mp*. Write a brief definition of both these terms.

Answers

1. Hans Leo Hassler was born in the year 1564 and died in 1612. This Lied is scored for soprano I, soprano II, alto, tenor, and bass.

2. The form of the first section is AA; the form of the second section is BB. The overall form of this piece of AABB.

3. The cadence at the end of the "A" section, mm. 13-14, is not a perfect authentic cadence because the c-sharp is in the soprano rather than the tonic a. The final cadence is a perfect authentic cadence; the bass moves V-I and a' is in the soprano.

4. *Andante* (ahn-dahn'-teh) suggests a moderate tempo—walking speed. *Mp,* or *mezzo piano* means moderately soft.

Activity

Divide the class into two or more groups. Look carefully at the English translation of the text. Based on your experience as a chorister, do you think vocal music should be sung in its original language or sung using an English translation? Write down the pros and cons of each and report them to the other group/s. Discuss whether or not one is more aesthetically pleasing than the other. Why? Why not?

Josquin Desprez's
2. "Ave Maria, Gratia Plena"
("Hail Mary, Full of Grace")

1. The motet (mo-TET) was one of the most frequently composed and one of the most expressive forms of the Renaissance. The wide variety of motet texts offered composers more opportunity for creative expression than did the fixed texts of the Mass Ordinary. From the information given you and from your work with Josquin's "Ave Maria," write a brief definition of the sixteenth-century motet.

2. Many characteristics of Josquin's style are present in this motet. One is the manner in which he varies the texture within a work. Imitative sections, that is, sections in which the voices enter in an imitative fashion, alternate with homophonic or chordal sections. The texture of the opening section of this motet is definitely _____; the texture at mm. 94-109 is more _____. Josquin also varied the texture by having voices sing in pairs, e.g., soprano and alto sing a phrase which is answered by tenor and bass. Where does this first occur in this motet? Is this technique used again? If so, where?

3. The voices enter in this motet in an imitative fashion. Imitation is defined as the restatement in close succession of the melody or theme in all the parts. Look at the beginning of this composition, and determine if all the voices enter with the interval of a fourth, as does the soprano. If all do, the imitation is said to be "real"; if not, the imitation is said to be "tonal." Circle your answer.

real   tonal

4. The *canon* was a favorite compositional device of Josquin and his contemporaries. A canon is a contrapuntal device in which a melody stated in one part is imitated strictly and entirely in another voice. Look carefully at m. 94. Since the canon begins in the soprano, in which voice is it strictly imitated?

Answers

1.   The motet is a choral composition based on a sacred Latin text and was performed in the
      Roman Catholic service, mainly at vespers, an evening service.

2.   The texture of the opening section is imitative. The voices enter with the same theme in
      descending order—soprano, alto, tenor, and bass.

      The texture at mm. 94-109 is more homophonic and chordal.

      The voices are first paired at mm. 31-39; soprano and alto are answered by tenor and bass.

      The voices are paired again on pages 12 and 13.

3.   All the voices enter with the same interval as the soprano. Therefore, the imitation is real.

4.   The canon is between the soprano and tenor. The tenor sings the same melody as the soprano,
      but it sings it five notes below, thus the canon in the tenor is a fifth below the soprano.

Activity
Sacred music is studied in schools for its greatness as a genre, not for religious purposes. What is
your definition of sacred music? What definition is given in a dictionary? As you study and perform
this section of sacred music, list some definite differences between sacred and secular music besides
the texts used. For example, are the rhythms more pronounced in secular music? Are the forms more
defined in sacred music? Cite specific examples.

Giovanni Pierluigi da Palestrina's "Kyrie" from *Missa Brevis*

1. The Mass, with the possible exception of the motet, constitutes some of the most beautiful and profound music of all time. The "Kyrie" which you have sung is the first movement of Palestrina's *Missa brevis*, that is, short Mass. As the name implies, this type of Mass was both shorter and simpler than the majority of the ones being composed during the sixteenth century. The *Mass Ordinary* has had a great influence upon all Western music and musicians, and the texts for the five items are always the same. Although you have sung only the first item of Palestrina's Mass, can you give a brief translation for each of the five parts of the Ordinary?

   Kyrie eleison   _____
   Gloria in Excelsis   _____
   Credo   _____
   Sanctus   _____
   Agnus Dei   _____

2. The melodies found in Palestrina's music, as well as in most Renaissance vocal music, are very singable. This is basically because they move by step, although skips are used for variety. This is especially true in Palestrina's music, since he was very much influenced by the smooth lines of Gregorian chant. When a melody moves mainly by step, it is said to be *conjunct*; when it moves mainly by skip, it is said to be *disjunct*. Look at your part in the "Kyrie." Is it basically conjunct or disjunct? Circle your conclusion.

                    conjunct   disjunct

3. The texture for each section of the "Kyrie" is imitative, that is, the melody stated in one voice is imitated by the others. This is most properly referred to as imitative counterpoint. In the "Christe" section, however, the voices are not strictly imitated, so the texture is most properly referred to as nonimitative counterpoint. Look at the first "Kyrie." The alto enters first with the theme. This is imitated next by the _____, then by the _____, and then by the _____. Are the entrances in the second "Kyrie" the same or different? In what order do they enter there? _____, _____, _____, and _____.

4. Considering each section of this Mass movement, and using letters, the form of the "Kyrie" is ___ ___ ___.

Answers

1.
Kyrie eleison	Lord, have mercy upon us.
Gloria in Excelsis	Glory to God in the highest.
Credo	I believe in one God. ·
Sanctus	Holy, holy, holy.
Agnus Dei	Lamb of God.

2. Taken as a whole, the melodies are all basically *conjunct*.

3. In the first "Kyrie," the voices enter alto, bass, soprano, and tenor. In the second "Kyrie," the voices enter from bottom to top: bass, tenor, alto, and soprano.

4. The form is ABC.

Activity

It is interesting to read and know the entire translations of the *Mass Ordinary* (called "Ordinary" because the text never changes). These texts have inspired composers for almost 20 centuries. Look up the translations in a music dictionary under *Mass*. Notice that the "Kyrie" is in Greek, while the other mass items are in Latin. The translations, of course, are in English.

Giovanni Pierluigi da Palestrina's "Agnus Dei" from *Missa Veni sponsa Christi*

1. The Mass, with the possible exception of the motet, was the most frequently composed form during the Renaissance. More often than not, composers based their Masses on a melody or an entire section of another composition, usually a motet, chanson, or madrigal. When entire sections were borrowed, the type of Mass was known as a Parody Mass. Palestrina's *Missa Veni sponsa Christi* is a Parody Mass because he borrowed entire sections from his motet, "Veni sponsa Christi" ("Come Bride of Christ") to use as a basis. Masses were named for the composition on which they were based. Now write a brief definition of Parody Mass and include why this Mass has the title it does.

2. Below is a segment of Gregorian chant on which Palestrina based his motet and Mass. Look at the beginning of the "Agnus Dei." In which two voices does it appear unchanged except rhythmically? In which two voices does it appear transposed?

Ve - ni spon - sa Chri - sti ac - ci - pe co - ro - nam.

quam ti - bi Do - mi - nus prae - pa - ra - vit in ae - ter - num.

Example 10. Antiphon: "Veni sponsa Christi."

The Gregorian chant appears unchanged in the _____ and _____ voices. It appears transposed in the _____ and _____ voices.

3. A canon is a contrapuntal device in which a melody stated in one part is imitated strictly and entirely in another voice. Look carefully at "Agnus Dei II." In which two voices does the canon appear?

The canon appears in the _____ and _____ voices.

4.   This Mass movement is based on the Mixolydian mode, which looks like the following:

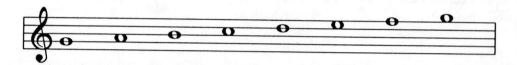

Example 11. Mixolydian mode.

The Mixolydian mode begins on ___ and ends on ___. Renaissance composers usually ended a composition in the lowest voice with the final or last note of the mode in which the composition was cast. What is the last note in the bass voice of the "Agnus Dei II"? Does Palestrina end this composition on the final of the Mixolydian mode? Write your conclusions below.

Answers

1.   A Parody Mass is a Mass based on entire sections of another composition, although much newly composed music is also present.

      Masses receive their names from the source of the borrowed material, usually a motet, chanson, madrigal, or segment of Gregorian chant.

2.   The Gregorian chant melody appears unchanged, except rhythmically, in the soprano and tenor. It is transposed down a perfect fifth in the alto and bass.

3.   The canon in the "Agnus Dei II" begins in the soprano and is answered in the *Quinta Pars*, or tenor II.

4.   The Mixolydian mode begins on g' and ends on g". The lowest note of the final chord is a "g." Palestrina ends this movement on the final of the Mixolydian mode.

Activity

Masses were written by composers well before the Renaissance, as well as into our century. If a recording is available of Palestrina's *Missa Veni sponsa Christi* (check your school and public libraries), listen to it and carefully listen for the texts. Also, notice the texture of each movement. Is the "Kyrie" imitative? Does the "Gloria" begin with a polyphonic or homophonic texture? What is the texture of the "Credo?" The "Sanctus?" As a general rule, the shorter the text, the more polyphonic and longer the composition; the longer texts are usually set in a homophonic texture with a syllabic text setting.

Orlando Gibbons's
"Why Art Thou So Heavy, O My Soul?"

1.   The English anthem evolved when the Church of England separated from the Roman Catholic Church in 1534. The early anthems differed from motets mainly in that English rather than Latin texts were used. Two types of anthems developed, and both were composed by the well-known English composer Orlando Gibbons. The first type was called a full anthem because the full choir sings throughout. The second type is known as a verse anthem; sections for full choir alternate with sections for soloists. The verse anthem also has a separate instrumental accompaniment. The anthem which you have sung by Gibbons is a _____ anthem because _____.

2.   Renaissance composers were very much aware of the texts they were setting to music. Three basic styles of text setting were used: *syllabic*, one syllable of text to each note or chord; *neumatic*, several notes to one syllable of text; and *melismatic*, numerous notes to one syllable of text. Which style of text setting did Gibbons use for his anthem? Is the text setting different in the last four measures? _____.

3.   The voices enter in this anthem in an imitative fashion. Imitation is defined as the restatement in close succession of the melody or theme in different parts. Look at the beginning of this composition and determine if all the voices enter with the same intervals as does the soprano. If so, the imitation is said to be "real"; if not, the imitation is said to be "tonal." Circle your conclusion.

    tonal imitation   real imitation

4.   The *plagal cadence* is frequently used in Renaissance music. From its frequent appearance at the end of church anthems, it became known also as the *amen cadence*. The plagal cadence has a IV-I progression in the bass. Look at the final cadence in Gibbons's anthem. Is it a plagal or perfect authentic cadence? Circle your conclusion and state your reason.

    perfect authentic cadence   plagal cadence

    _____

    _____

Answers

1.   Gibbons's "Why Art Thou So Heavy, O My Soul?" is a full anthem because the full choir sings throughout as opposed to the verse anthems in which soloists and instrumental accompaniment are employed as well as the choir.

2.   The text setting is syllabic throughout except for the final *Amen* section. The *Amen* section is more melismatic than syllabic.

3.   All the voices enter with the same intervals as the soprano for the first phrase of text. Therefore, the imitation is real.

4.   The final cadence is a plagal cadence. The IV-I progression in the bass, rather than V-I, makes it a plagal rather than a perfect authentic cadence.

Activity

Students will be divided into two groups. Each group will find out more information about full and verse anthems by English Renaissance composers. Go to libraries and record stores, consult dictionaries and encyclopedias, such as *The New Grove Dictionary of Music and Musicians,* edited by Stanley Sadie and published by Grove's Dictionaries of Music, Inc., Washington, DC (if your library doesn't have it, ask for it!). Each group will report its findings after one week of research. Perhaps some of this excellent music has been sung by your church choir. Ask the choir director. Perhaps you could find another full or verse anthem for study and performance in your choral class!

Michael Praetorius's
"Psallite"
("Sing Your Psalms")

1. This joyous Christmas piece is a chorale motet. Protestant German composers at the end of the sixteenth century began to use chorales as the basis for many of their compositions. The "Psallite" comes from a collection of some 1,200 chorale-based compositions published by the German composer, Michael Praetorius. This chorale motet is scored for four voices which, reading from top to bottom, are _____, _____, _____, and _____. The voices enter in an imitative fashion. The first voice to enter is the _____, the second is the _____, the third is the _____, and the last is the _____.

2. The variety of textures used in this motet makes it especially interesting. Sections in which the voices enter in an imitative fashion are altered with homophonic or chordal sections. The texture is further varied by having the voices sing in pairs; soprano and alto sing a phrase which is answered by tenor and bass. Look at the first section (8 measures) of this motet. In which specific measures do you find imitation, homophony, and pairing of voices?

3. When all the voices in a composition move in the same rhythm, the composition is said to be *homorhythmic*, literally "same rhythm." When this occurs, the text setting is usually *syllabic*, one note or chord is given to each syllable of text. Look through "Psallite" and find those sections which are both homorhythmic and syllabic.

4. This composition falls into three main sections. Is the first section different from the second? Are the first and last sections the same or different? Consider each section and use letters to indicate the form. The form is ___ ___ ___.

Answers

1. "Psallite" is scored for soprano, alto, tenor, and bass. The voices enter in an imitative fashion. The tenor begins; this part is imitated by the bass, which is followed by soprano and alto.

2. The texture of the first two measures is imitative. Measures 6-8 are chordal. The voices are paired in mm. 4 and 5.

3. This composition is syllabic throughout. Homorhythm and syllabic text setting occur in mm. 6-8, as well as the last three measures of the piece.

4. The form is ABA.

Activity

What are some of the basic truths you have learned about Renaissance vocal music, its style, structure, and performance? Make a list under each category.

Do you feel that you sing with more understanding as a result of going through "The Performer's Workbook?" A quote at the beginning of *The Harvard Dictionary of Music,* edited by the German musicologist Willi Apel in 1969, states that "if you want to understand the invisible, look carefully at the visible" (p. xviii). By so doing, the art of music is less mysterious and our work with it is more intelligent and meaningful. As the Introduction stated, sing, *learn,* and enjoy it!

Bibliography

Abraham, Gerald, ed. *The New Oxford History of Music. The Age of Humanism 1540-1630.* Vol. IV. London: Oxford University Press, 1968.

Adler, Guido, ed. *Denkmäler der Tonkunst in Österreich.* Vienna: Artaria and Company, 1894.

Amcot, François. *History of the Mass.* Translated by Lancelot C. Sheppard. New York: Hawthorn Books, 1959.

Andrews, H. K. *An Introduction to the Technique of Palestrina.* London: Novello, 1968.

Apel, Willi, ed. *The Harvard Dictionary of Music.* Cambridge, MA: The Belknap Press of Harvard University Press, 1969.

Arcadelt, Jacob. *Corpus mensurabilis musicae 31.* Edited by Albert Seay. Rome: American Institute of Musicology, 1948.

Arnold, Denis. *Marenzio.* London: Oxford University Press, 1965.

Baker's Biographical Dictionary of Music. 8th ed. Edited by N. Slonimsky. New York: G. Schirmer, 1991.

Bartle, Barton K. *Computer Software in Music and Music Education: A Guide.* Metuchen, NJ: The Scarecrow Press, 1987.

Blume, Friedrich. *Renaissance and Baroque Music: A Comprehensive Survey.* Translated by M. D. Herter Norton. New York: W. W. Norton & Company, Inc., 1967.

Brown, David. *Thomas Weelkes.* New York: F. A. Praeger, 1969.

Bruner, Jerome. *The Process of Education.* Cambridge, MA: Harvard University Press, 1978.

Bukofzer, Manfred F. *Studies in Medieval and Renaissance Music.* New York: W. W. Norton & Company, 1950.

Burney, Charles. *A General History of Music*, 4 vols., London, 1776-89.New ed. by Frank Mercer, 2 vols., New York: Harcourt, Brace & World, 1935; reprinted, New York: Dover Publications, 1960.

Byrd, William. *Collected Works*. Edited by Edmund H. Fellowes. 20 vols. London: Stainer and Bell, 1937-1950.

_____. *Psalmes, Songs and Sonnets*, 1588. Ed. by E. H. Fellowes. London: Stainer and Bell, 1920.

Chater, James M. *Luca Marenzio and the Italian Madrigal, 1577-1593*. Ann Arbor, MI: UMI Research Press, [ca. 1981].

Coates, Henry. *Palestrina*. London: Dent, 1938.

Cohen, Helen Louise. *Lyric Forms from France: Their History and Their Use*. New York: Harcourt, Brace & Co., 1922.

Colvig, Richard and Coover, James. *Medieval and Renaissance Music on Long-Playing Records, Detroit Studies in Music Bibliography*, Number 6. Detroit: Information Service, Inc., 1964.

Dart, R. Thurston. *The Interpretation of Music*. London: Hutchinson's University Library, 1954.

Davison, Archibald T. and Apel, Willi, eds. *Historical Anthology of Music*. Vol. I, 2nd ed. Cambridge, MA: Harvard University Press, 1949.

Des Prez, Josquin. *Werke*. Edited by Albert Smijers. Leipzig: Kistner und Siegel, 1925.

Donnington, Robert. *The Interpretation of Early Music*. London: Faber and Faber, Ltd., 1963.

Dottin, Georges. *La chanson française de la Renaissance*. Paris: Presses universitaires de France, 1984.

Dunn, Rita and Dunn, Kenneth. *Teaching Students through Their Individual Learning Styles: A Practical Approach*. Englewood Cliffs, NJ: Prentice-Hall, Inc., 1978.

Einstein, Alfred. *The Golden Age of the Madrigal*. New York: G. Schirmer, 1942.

_____. *The Italian Madrigal*. 3 vols. Princeton: Princeton University Press, 1949.

Expert, Henry, ed. *Les Maîtres musiciens de la Renaissance française*. Paris: Alphonse Leduc, 1894-1908.

Fellowes, Edmund Horace. *English Cathedral Music*. 5th ed. London: Methuen, 1969.

____. *The English Madrigal*. London: Oxford University Press, 1947.

____. *The English Madrigal Composers*. Oxford: The Clarendon Press, 1921.

____, ed. *The English Madrigal School*. 36 vols. London: Stainer and Bell, Ltd., 1923.

The 4MAT®System. Part A: Introduction to Learning Styles. Excel, Inc., 200 West Station Street, Barrington, AL, 60010, 1991.

The 4Mat®System. Part B: Introduction to Right/Left Processing and the 4MAT® Model. Excel, Inc., 200 West Station Street, Barrington, AL, 60010, 1991.

Fowler, Charles B. "Music Education through Performance," The Instrumentalist (November 1964).

Gardner, Howard. *Frames of Mind: The Theory of Multiple Intelligences*. New York: Basic Books Inc., Publishers, 1983.

Grout, Donald Jay. *A History of Western Music*. 4th ed. New York: W. W. Norton & Co., Inc., 1988.

Haar, James, ed. *Chanson and Madrigal, 1480-1530: Studies in Comparison and Contrast*. Cambridge, MA: Harvard University Press, 1964.

Hale, John R., et al. *Great Ages of Man: Renaissance*. New York: Time-Life Books, 1965.

Harman, Alec. *Man and His Music: Mediaeval and Early Renaissance Music*. New York: Schocken Books, 1962.

____. and Milner, Anthony. *Man and His Music: Late Renaissance and Baroque Music*. New York: Schocken Books, 1962.

Hassler, Hans Leo. *Sämtliche Werke*. Vol. 2. *Canzonette von 1590 und Neue Teutsche Gesäng von 1596*. Edited by Rudolf Schwartz. Wiesbaden: Breitkopf und Härtel,

1961.

Hoffer, Charles R. *Teaching Music in the Secondary Schools*. 4th ed. Belmont, CA: Wadsworth Publishing Co., Inc., 1991.

_____. "Teaching Useful Knowledge in Rehearsal," *Music Educators Journal* 52, no. 5 (April-May, 1966).

_____ and Anderson, Donald K. *Performing Music with Understanding*. Edition, Orange and Green. Belmont, CA: Wadsworth Publishing Co., Inc., 1970, 1971.

Hughes, Dom Anselm, ed. *The History of Music in Sound: Ars Nova and the Renaissance, ca. 1300-1540*. Vol. III. London: Oxford University Press, 1953.

_____ and Abraham, Gerald, eds. *The New Oxford History of Music. Ars Nova and the Renaissance, 1300-1540*. Vol. III. London: Oxford University Press, 1960.

Huray, Peter le and Daniel, Ralph T. *Music and Reformation in England, 1549-1660*. London: Stainer and Bell, Ltd., 1972.

Isaac, Heinrich. *Weltliche Werke*. Edited by Johannes Wolf. 2nd ed. Graz: Akademische Druck-u. Verlagsanstalt, 1959.

Jeppesen, Knud. *The Style of Palestrina and the Dissonance*. London: Oxford University Press, 1927.

Kerman, Joseph. *The Elizabethan Madrigal*. New York: Galaxy Music Corp., 1962.

Kreloff, Herschel Mayer. Abstract of "Instructional and Performance Materials for Teaching the Historical Development of Musical Style to the High School Band Student," *Dissertation Abstracts*, XXXII/04. Ph.D. dissertation, University of Arizona, 1971.

Lang, Paul Henry. *Music in Western Civilization*. New York: W. W. Norton & Co., Inc., 1941.

Laughlin, Sister M. Donalda. "Developing Basic Musicianship through the Study of Medieval and Early Renaissance Music," Ph.D. dissertation, University of

Southern California, 1967.

Lowinsky, Edward E. *Cipriano de Rore's Venus Motet: Its Poetic and Pictorial Sources.* Provo, UT: Brigham Young University, [ca. 1986].

_____. *Secret Chromatic Art in the Netherlands Motet.* Translated by Carl Buchman. New York: Columbia University Press, 1946.

_____. *Tonality and Atonality in Sixteenth-Century Music.* Berkeley: University of California Press, 1961.

Marenzio, Luca. *The Secular Works.* Edited by Steven Ledbetter and Patricia Myers. New York: Broude Bros., 1977-

Mark, Michael L. *Contemporary Music Education.* 2nd ed. New York: Schirmer Books, 1986.

Martin, James Gautier. Abstract of "An Application of Bruner's Theory of Instruction to Selected Features of Renaissance Choral Music," *Dissertation Abstracts,* XXXIV/05A. Ph.D. dissertation, University of Texas at Austin, 1973.

Mathis, William Stephen. Abstract of "Thirty-six Selected Choral Works of the Sixteenth Century Adapted and Annotated for Performance by Non-Professional Choral Groups," *Disseration Abstracts,* XII/05. Ph.D. dissertation, Florida State University, 1952.

Meyer, Leonard B. "Some Remarks on Value and Greatness in Music," *Perspectives in Music Education.* Source Book III. Music Educators National Conference, 1966.

MMCP Synthesis. Report of the Manhattanville Music Curriculum Program. Edited by Ronald B. Thomas. Elmira, N Y : Media, Inc., 1965-1970.

Morley, Thomas. *A Plaine and Easie Introduction to Practicall Musicke,* 1597. Edited by Alec Harman. New York: Norton, 1973.

____. *The First Book of Balletts for Five Voices,* 1595. Edited by Edward F. Rimbault. London: Musical Antiquarian Society, 1842.

Music in Our Schools: A Search for Improvement. Report of the Yale Seminar on Music Education. Edited by Claude V. Palisca. Washington, DC: U.S. Government

Printing Office, 1964.

The New Grove Dictionary of Music and Musicians. Edited by Stanley Sadie. 20 vols. Washington, DC: Grove's Dictionaries of Music, Inc., 1980.

The New Harvard Dictionary of Music. Edited by Don Michael Randel. Cambridge, MA: The Belknap Press of Harvard University Press, 1986.

Palestrina, Giovanni Pierluigi da. *Werke.* Edited by Franz X. Haberl et al. 33 vols. Leipzig: Breitkopf und Härtel, 1862-1900.

Parrish, Carl, ed. *A Treasury of Early Music: An Anthology of Masterworks of the Middle Ages, the Renaissance, and the Baroque Era.* New York: W. W. Norton & Co., Inc., 1958.

_____ and Ohl, John F., eds. *Masterpieces of Music Before 1750: An Anthology of Musical Examples from Gregorian Chant to J. S. Bach.* New York: W. W. Norton & Co., Inc., 1951.

Picker, Martin, ed. *The Chanson Albums of Marguerite of Austria.* Berkeley: University of California Press, 1965.

Praetorius, Michael. *Gesamtausgabe der musikalischen Werke.* Edited by F. Blume, W. Gurlitt and A. Mendelssohn. 20 vols. Wolfenbüttel: Gikallpaeyer Verlag, 1928-40.

_____. *Syntagma Musicum.* Vols. 1 and 2. Wolfenbüttel, 1615-1620; New York: Bärenreiter, 1958; English translation by Harold Blumenfeld. New York: Bärenreiter, 1962.

Reese, Gustave. *Music in the Renaissance.* 2nd ed. New York: W. W. Norton & Co., Inc., 1959.

Reimer, Bennett. *A Philosophy of Music Education.* Englewood Cliffs, NJ: Prentice-Hall, Inc., [ca. 1989].

Robertson, Alec and Stevens, Denis. *The Pelican History of Music: Renaissance and*

Baroque. Vol. II. Harmondsworth, Middlesex: Penguin Books, 1950.

Roche, Jerome. *The Madrigal.* 2nd ed. New York: Oxford University Press, 1990.

_____. *Palestrina.* London: Oxford University Press, 1971.

Rore, Cipriano de. *Corpus mensurabilis musicae 14.* Edited by Bernhard Meier. Vols. 3 & 4. Rome: American Institute of Musicology, 1959.

Rousseau, Jean-Jacques. *Dictionnaire de musique,* 1768. New York: Johnson Reprint Corp., 1969.

Sanvoisin, Michael, ed. *Balletti a cinque voci,* 1591. Paris: Heugel & Cie., 1968.

Saunders, Stanley. "A Study to Adapt Selected Instrumental and Vocal Compositions of the Renaissance as a Practical Guide for Secondary School Use," *Dissertation Abstracts* XXXI/10. Ph.D. dissertation, University of Oregon, 1970.

Scholes, Percy A. *The Oxford Companion to Music.* 8th ed. London: Oxford University Press, 1950.

Scott, Charles Kennedy. *Madrigal Singing.* London: Oxford University Press, 1931.

Seay, Albert, ed. *Thirty Chansons for Three and Four Voices from Attaingnant's Collection, Collegium Musicum* 2. New Haven: Yale University Dept. of Music, 1960.

Senfl, Ludwig. *Sämtliche Werke.* Wolfenbüttel: Möseler, 1949 - .

Sermisy, Claudin de. *Corpus mensurabilis musicae 52.* Edited by G. Allaire and I. Cazeaux. Rome: American Institute of Musicology, 1970- .

Sparks, Edgar H. *Cantus Firmus in Mass and Motet, 1420-1520.* Berkeley: University of California Press, 1968.

Strunk, Oliver, ed. *Source Readings in Music History: The Renaissance.* New York: W. W. Norton & Co., Inc., 1965.

Student Learning Styles and Brain Behavior. National Association of Secondary School Principals, 1986.

Thomson, James C. *Music through the Renaissance*. Dubuque, IA: Wm. C. Brown Co., 1968.

Tudor Church Music. Edited by P. C. Buck, E. H. Fellowes, A. Ramsbotham, R. R. Terry, and S. Townsend Warner. 10 vols. London: Oxford University Press, 1922-1929. Vol. 4. *Orlando Gibbons*.

Walvoord, Barbara. *Helping Students to Write Well: A Guide for Teachers in All Disciplines*. New York: Modern Language Association of America,1986.

Weinandt, Elwyn A. *Choral Music of the Church*. New York: The Free Press, 1965.

White, Robert Charles, Jr. Abstract of "A Source-Book for the Study and Performance of Renaissance Choral Music Including Application to the Secondary-School Level," *Dissertation Abstracts*, XXXI/01. Ph.D. dissertation, Columbia University, 1968.

Whitton, Kenneth S. *Lieder: An Introduction to German Song*. London: J. McRae; New York: Franklin Watts, 1984.

Wold, Milo and Cykler, Edmund. *An Outline History of Music*. Dubuque, IA: Wm. C. Brown Co., 1963.

Yonge, Nicholas. *Musica transalpina*, London, 1588. Introduction by Denis Stevens. Westmead, Farnborough, Hants., England: Gregg Publishers Limited, 1972.

About the Author

Frances R. Poe received the B. Music degree from the University of Georgia and the M.M. and Ph.D. degrees from Indiana University. She has taught general music and choral classes to grades K-12, and undergraduate and graduate classes in music education and music history. She has been on the music faculties of Bemidji State University, the University of Rhode Island, and Westminster Choir College, the School of Music of Rider College, where she has served as Head of Westminster's Music Education Department. Dr. Poe founded and directed both the URI Madrigal Singers and Westminster's *Collegium Musicum,* groups devoted to the study and performance of Renaissance vocal and instrumental music. She has served as Director of Music in churches in Georgia, Florida, Pennsylvania, and New Jersey. Dr. Poe is included in *Who's Who Among Outstanding Musicians, Who's Who Among Outstanding Educators,* and *Who's Who Among Outstanding Women.*